THOMAS JEFFERSON'S

Poplar Forest

A PRIVATE PLACE

Poplar Forest today.

ISBN 0-9667169-1-4

CONTENTS

A Tulip Poplar Bloom

Written & Researched By
JOAN L. HORN

LEARNING ABOUT
JEFFERSON AT
POPLAR FOREST

Thomas Jefferson was a person of relentless curiosity. Fascinated with the world around him, he sought to learn about almost everything he encountered. The world too has long exhibited a fascination with Jefferson. As his Pulitzer Prize-winning biographer Dumas Malone has written, "By the very contradictions of his subtle and complex personality, of his bold mind and highly sensitive nature, Jefferson has both vexed and fascinated all who have attempted to interpret him." Poplar Forest presents us with a unique opportunity to understand this exceptional person anew.

Poplar Forest was an important part of Jefferson's life: a private retreat, situated far from the public scrutiny and demands on his time of which he had grown so weary. It was his most personal architectural creation and landscape, a place where he came to find rest and leisure, to rekindle his creativity, and to enjoy private family time. Poplar Forest was also a working plantation, critical to Jefferson's efforts as a farmer. The lives of the enslaved men and women who worked for Jefferson are an important part of the Poplar Forest story.

Poplar Forest offers an intimate portrait of Jefferson not just because of its unique role in his private life. Here, the visitor's experience is also intimate. By allowing ourselves to get close to Jefferson, we see him not so much as a historical figure who awes us, but more as a person like ourselves. The house is remarkably

By the very contradictions of his subtle and complex personality, of his bold mind and highly sensitive nature, Jefferson has both vexed and fascinated all who have attempted to interpret him.

—DUMAS MALONE

accessible. Inside, you literally see behind the walls. So, too, do you see behind the "great man" façade of Jefferson himself; he becomes a very real example of how we, too, can live lives of curiosity and creativity.

Because our exploration of Poplar Forest is so young, beginning in earnest in 1987, new discoveries are happening every day. Ongoing archaeological excavation and architectural restoration are part of the visitor's experience of Jefferson. You might see a mason laying brick just as Jefferson's masons did. You might find yourself looking into an archaeological dig as we continue to uncover Jefferson's life here. There is still so much to learn, restore, and preserve. As it was for those who saved other major American landmarks like Mount Vernon and Monticello, the challenge and excitement of saving and restoring Poplar Forest falls to our generation, so that our children and grandchildren may learn from it too.

We hope this book will capture some of the fascinating and dynamic experience Poplar Forest offers. For those who have not visited, we hope it will inspire you to come. For those who have, we hope it will enhance your visit and inspire you to return and take part in our continuing exploration. Most of all, we hope it will help you learn about Thomas Jefferson, just as Jefferson was so often learning himself.

Lynn A. Beebe

Lynn A. Beebe
Executive Director

The whole site is Jefferson's last dramatic marriage of classical art with the American wilderness . . . a masterpiece of Jefferson's art and a revelation of his mind.

—GARRY WILLS, HISTORIAN

The Tomahawk Creek runs through Poplar Forest .

1772 First daughter, Martha Jefferson, born

1776 Writes the Declaration of Independence

1779 Elected governor of Virginia

1743	Born at Shadwell, Albemarle County, Virginia, April 13.
1760	Enters College of William & Mary in Williamsburg.
1767	Begins practicing law in Albemarle County.
1768	Elected to the Virginia House of Burgesses. Construction begins on house at Monticello.
1772	Marries Martha Wayles Skelton in January. Daughter Martha born in September.
1773	Inherits Poplar Forest and visits for the first time.
1775	Elected to the Continental Congress.
1776	Writes Declaration of Independence.
1777	Drafts Virginia Statute for Religious Freedom (passed by the Virginia General Assembly in 1786).
1778	Daughter Mary (Maria) born in August.
1779	Elected governor of Virginia.
1781	Brings family to Poplar Forest during the American Revolution. While there, works on *Notes on the State of Virginia*.
1782	Wife Martha dies.
1784	Appointed minister to France. Stays for five years.

1787	Published *Notes on the State of Virginia*.
1790	Appointed secretary of state by President George Washington.
1796	Elected vice president of the United States under John Adams.
1801	Begins first term as president of the United States.

1801 Begins term as president of the United States

1803	Louisiana Purchase concluded. Lewis and Clark expedition launched.
1804	Daughter Maria Jefferson Eppes dies.
1806	Construction begins on the octagonal house and ornamental grounds at Poplar Forest.
1809	Leaves Washington, D.C. following his second term as president. Stays at his house at Poplar Forest for the first time.

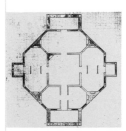
1806 Construction begins on retreat at Poplar Forest

1816	Finishes interior plastering of walls. Granddaughters visit for the first time.
1819	Founds the University of Virginia.
1823	Visits Poplar Forest for the final time. Grandson Francis Eppes and his wife move into the house.
1826	Dies July 4 at Monticello at age 83. Francis Eppes inherits the Poplar Forest house and 1,074 acres of land.

1819 Founds the University of Virginia

A RETREAT

THOMAS JEFFERSON AND POPLAR FOREST

*I have an excellent house there . . .
am comfortably fixed and attended,
have a few good neighbors, and pass
my time there in tranquility and
retirement much adapted to my age
and indolence.*

—THOMAS JEFFERSON TO WILLIAM SHORT,
NOVEMBER 24, 1821

In April 1806, during his second term as president of the United States, Thomas Jefferson confided in a letter to his friend Elizabeth Trist, "I am preparing an occasional retreat in Bedford where I expect to settle some of my grandchildren." The property was a tract of land, more than 4,000 acres, that he had owned for over thirty years but had visited just four times—a plantation, worked by about thirty of his slaves, known as Poplar Forest.

Under the circumstances, Jefferson's undertaking was extraordinary: his already serious financial straits were worsening. As president of the United States, he had little leisure to design a house and landscape and to supervise their creation. He was also just then completing Monticello, his primary residence situated atop a mountain in Albemarle County, which had been thirty years in the making.

This new house represented a powerful idea to Jefferson: weary from years of public service, he sought to create a harmonious, tranquil place for himself. As one who delighted in architecture, in "putting up and pulling down," he also used the opportunity to create one last personal masterpiece.

Jefferson's Efforts to Build a Retreat

Jefferson had, in fact, attempted to establish a retreat for himself numerous times throughout his life.

As governor of Virginia, Jefferson used to visit Elk Hill, another plantation he had inherited from his father-in-law, where he stayed for a month at a time in a brick house. During the Revolutionary War, Lord Cornwallis camped at, then destroyed, Elk Hill. Jefferson sold the property in 1793 and little is known about it.

During his years in Paris, Jefferson often retreated for a week or more to a monastery on Mont Calvaire, where the brothers let paying guests stay to refresh body and soul.

Serving as secretary of state in Philadelphia, then the nation's capital, Jefferson gave instructions to construct a small outbuilding at his rented townhouse as a private space where he "might have a place to retire & write in" when he "wished to be unseen & undisturbed." When the workmen mistakenly installed windows rather than a skylight, Jefferson found the space useless as a study.

From the parlor, doors opened onto a porch where Jefferson could view the South Lawn.

From 1809 until three years before his death in 1826, Jefferson visited Poplar Forest frequently. By his own testament, it was the peaceful place he had envisioned, a place, he once wrote, where he found "the solitude of a hermit."

Sold after his death, greatly altered, and fallen into disrepair, Poplar Forest is today being restored. It is emerging as a stunning environment where architecture and landscape are seamlessly intertwined. The study of Poplar Forest is shedding new light on Jefferson, his creativity, his curiosity, and his private world.

Who Was Thomas Jefferson?

Jefferson's record of public service is extraordinary: he was author of the Virginia Statute for Religious Freedom, governor of Virginia, minister to France, first secretary of state, second vice president, and third president of the United States. In his retirement, he founded the University of Virginia. He is best known for writing the Declaration of Independence, a document so enduring that it continues to be invoked around the world by people striving for liberty, equality, and the right to self-government.

But what was Jefferson like as a person? Many aspects of his personality point to his need for privacy. Unlike many of the Founding Fathers, Jefferson was not a great public orator, but was shy, the "silent member" of the Continental Congress. The personal criticisms that go along with public life pained him, and he frequently articulated the same desire "to detach myself from public life, which I never loved, to retire to the bosom of my family my friends, my farm and books, which I have always loved."

As early as age thirty-six, during his tenure as governor of Virginia, Jefferson began to think about retiring from public life. Retirement did not come until 1809, however, when Jefferson was sixty-five years old.

I continue in the enjoyment of good health, take much exercise, and make frequent journeys to Bedford, the only journies I now take, or ever expect to take.

—THOMAS JEFFERSON TO JOHN BARNES, JANUARY 10, 1811

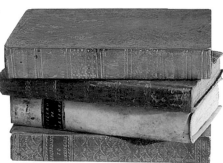

Music

Describing music as "the favorite passion of my soul," Jefferson considered music a "delightful recreation" throughout his life. As a child he learned to play the violin and continued to play and listen to that instrument until his later years. His family often described his singing. His granddaughter remembered "his singing as we journeyed along" on their trips to Poplar Forest.

Jefferson owned several violins. He acquired a piano and a guitar for his family, and bought each of his daughters a Kirkman harpsichord. His extensive collection of music showed an interest in both vocal and instrumental music. Ellen Randolph wrote to her mother about how she missed her music at Poplar Forest. In 1819, Francis Eppes offered Jefferson Maria's harpsichord for the family's use at Poplar Forest. Having been stored with the Eppes family after Maria's death in 1804, Jefferson found it in poor condition and had it transported to Monticello to be repaired. It was readied to go to Poplar Forest in 1821, but the records do not show if it ever arrived. Jefferson purchased this cittern, or English guitar, for his granddaughter Virginia, a visitor to Poplar Forest.

He described his feelings, "Never did a prisoner, released from his chains, feel such relief as I shall on shaking off the shackles of power."

In his time out of the public spotlight, Jefferson pursued an astonishing array of interests, from math and the natural sciences to classical history and Native American culture. Not truly an inventor, he loved new technologies and often improved on items already in existence, such as the copying machine known as the polygraph. (He kept one polygraph at Monticello and another at Poplar Forest.) He read in six languages besides English, including Greek and Latin, and amassed one of early America's greatest libraries, keeping nearly seven hundred volumes at Poplar Forest alone. He was a talented architect and avid gardener. He considered himself a farmer by profession and was continually searching for more progressive ways to work his plantations. He often wished for more private time to pursue these interests.

Jefferson is known for his sophisticated taste. He loved art, music, fine wine, and French cuisine. Having visited the finest homes in Paris, he thought nothing of staying at the modest country inns on his journeys between Monticello and Poplar Forest. His letters reveal that he enjoyed the simple life he found in Bedford County.

Jefferson also enjoyed private time with his grandchildren there. He never remarried after the death of his wife. Their surviving family—daughters, Martha and Maria, and their twelve children—became his refuge and comfort.

Monticello bustled with activity. This watercolor by Jane Braddick Peticolas, made one year before Jefferson's death, shows his grandson George Wythe Randolph rolling a hoop on the west lawn.

Visitors at Monticello

For privacy at Monticello, Jefferson designed a suite of rooms—bedchamber, study, greenhouse, and library—that was rarely entered by others. Nevertheless, as his granddaughter Ellen recollected, "The crowd at Monticello of friends and strangers . . . wearied and harassed him in the end." His daughter Martha, her husband, and their eleven children all lived there. It was the norm for friends, relatives, and even distant acquaintances traveling through Virginia to stay overnight. Jefferson's granddaughters remembered two particularly abusive guests: one who stayed for six weeks each year with as many as six children

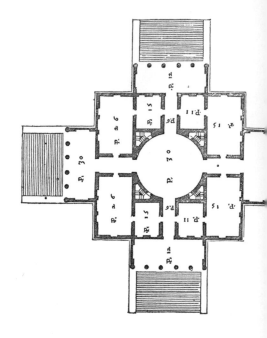

I read nothing, therefore, but of the heroes of Troy ... of Pompey and Caesar, and of Augustus too ... I slumber without fear, and review in my dreams the visions of antiquity.

—Thomas Jefferson to Nathaniel Macon, January 12, 1819

Thomas Jefferson was one of the intellectual leaders of the Enlightenment in America. The philosophy, history, and culture of ancient Greece and Rome provided an ideal to which many Enlightenment thinkers aspired. The American system of government, for example, was built on ancient principles of democracy and republicanism.

The harmonious, geometric buildings of neoclassical architecture, such as the Maison Carrée (pictured below), a Roman temple Jefferson admired while visiting France, expressed these ideals visually. As an architect, Jefferson pioneered the classical style in America.

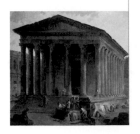

in tow and another who arrived with four children and bore a fifth at Monticello. Even worse, complete strangers ascended the mountain to glimpse the "Sage of Monticello."

With his home "considered as among the curiosities of the neighborhood," Poplar Forest became his escape: "I have neither strength nor spirits to encounter such a stream of strangers from day to day, and must therefore avoid it by obeying the necessary call of my concerns in Bedford to which place I shall set out tomorrow morning."

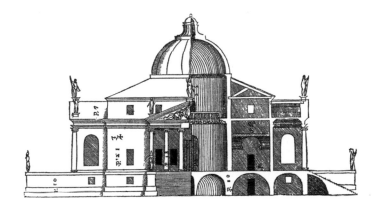

■ Andrea Palladio's Villa Rotunda. Jefferson looked to Palladio's ideas in designing his own villa retreat.

The Idea of the Villa

Poplar Forest was not simply a response to Jefferson's need for privacy. Characteristically, it was also the embodiment of a classical idea: the Roman villa retreat. Since antiquity, the villa has remained remarkably consistent in form and purpose: a home in the country designed for pleasure and repose, a place where owner and guests can forget the cares of the everyday world.

Andrea Palladio, the great Renaissance architect who strongly influenced Jefferson, wrote that "the ancient sages commonly used to retire to such places." At a villa, he went on, one "could easily attain to as much happiness as can be attained here below." Jefferson's Poplar Forest is a quintessential villa, perhaps the first in America.

The Genesis of an Idea

When Jefferson visited Poplar Forest in 1801, a rainstorm left him cooped up in the overseer's house—with numerous dogs and children. Jefferson spent his time—in what was undoubtedly a cramped and noisy setting—computing how long it would take to pay the national debt. It was then that he began to realize the advantages of building a more tranquil place for himself. Five years later, construction on the house and grounds at Poplar Forest began.

Given the many obstacles to its creation, Jefferson's decision to build a retreat may, on the surface, seem surprising. Given his need for privacy, his desire for an idyllic place, his love of architecture and landscape design, and his awareness of the peace this place could offer him, it instead seems, upon reflection, inevitable.

What did Jefferson look like?

Jefferson was 6 feet 2½ inches tall. As a young man he had sandy red hair and a freckled complexion. George Flower, a visitor from England, met the seventy-three-year-old Jefferson at Poplar Forest in 1816. He left the following description:

Mr. Jefferson's figure was rather majestic: tall (over six feet), thin, and rather high-shouldered: manners simple, kind, and courteous. His dress, in color and form, was quaint and old fashioned, plain and neat—a dark pepper-and-salt coat, cut in the old quaker fashion, with a single row of large metal buttons, knee-breeches, gray-worsted stockings, shoes fastened by large metal buckles.

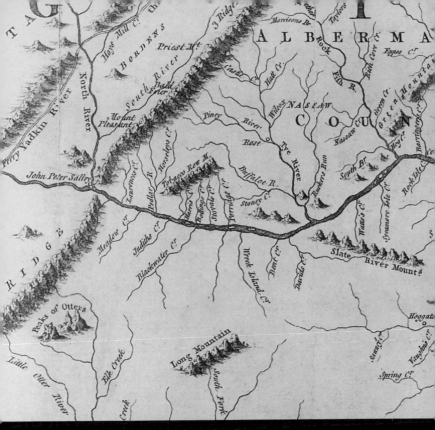

In June 1781, during the Revolutionary War, the British officer Lieutenant Colonel Banastre Tarleton charged west toward Charlottesville at breakneck speed. The goal of his surprise raid: to capture the governor of Virginia, Thomas Jefferson.

Jack Jouett, stopping in at Cuckoo Tavern in Louisa, Virginia, overheard British soldiers discussing their plan. A brave and skilled rider himself, Jouett raced to Monticello. According to

legend, Jefferson fortified him with Madeira wine before sending him off to warn members of the Virginia legislature staying nearby. After sending his family ahead, Jefferson himself escaped to Poplar Forest.

Jefferson, Martha, and their two young girls probably stayed with the overseer in what would have been a two-room house. When Jefferson fell from his horse Caractacus, the uncomfortable stay was

prolonged nearly two months. Removed from the world with little to do, Jefferson began drafting his only published book, *Notes on the State of Virginia*.

Poplar Forest was located between the Peaks of Otter and Blackwater Creek, in the lower left-hand corner of the map above.

The house at Poplar Forest.

View from beneath the portico on the south side of the house.

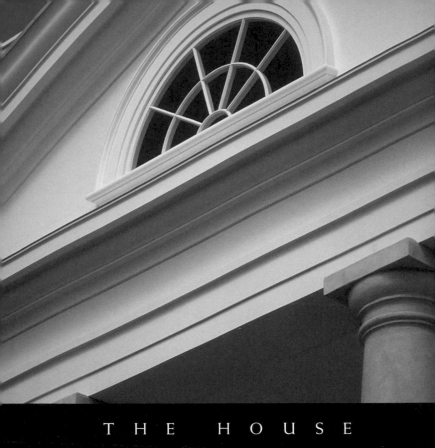

THE HOUSE

DESIGNING AND BUILDING THE POPLAR FOREST RESIDENCE

T homas Jefferson was America's first great native-born architect. Though classicism was his foundation, his distinctly American buildings incorporate a "melting pot" of design ideas. At Poplar Forest, elements from ancient, Renaissance Palladian, and eighteenth-century French architecture, as well as British and Virginian design, fuse into a harmonious whole.

By the time Jefferson constructed his retreat at Poplar Forest, he was in his sixties. He had one final opportunity to synthesize all that he had learned, and no one to please but himself. How did he choose to shape this very personal environment? The house is highly idealistic in concept with only a few concessions to practicality, and it is so perfectly suited to Jefferson alone that later owners found it difficult to inhabit.

Jefferson's perseverance in constructing the house, despite significant challenges, testifies to his unflagging optimism and idealism. It also suggests how much Poplar Forest meant to him.

Jefferson's Approach to Architecture

There never was a Palladio here even in private hands till I brought one . . . I send you my portable edition . . . it contains only the 1st book on the orders which is the essential part.
—THOMAS JEFFERSON TO JAMES OLDHAM, DECEMBER 24, 1804

Architectural Achievements

As a young man, Jefferson abhorred the architecture of Virginia and set himself the task of upgrading it. Besides Poplar Forest, the Virginia State Capitol, his home Monticello, and the University of Virginia are considered to be his masterpieces. He also influenced the planning of Washington, D.C.

In all of his designs, Jefferson fused ancient and modern to create a distinctly American architecture. His public work has been extremely influential. His design for the Virginia State Capitol, (pictured below) for example, was based on an ancient Roman temple. This style subsequently became the norm for civic buildings in America.

There were no architecture schools in colonial Virginia, so Jefferson learned architecture from books. His "bible" was Andrea Palladio's *The Four Books of Architecture,* which taught him the rules of classical design. Jefferson also looked to his contemporary world for ideas. His five-year tenure in France was one of the most intellectually stimulating times of his life. He was "violently smitten" with the architecture there, finding it not only elegant, but full of "modern" conveniences, which he later adopted at Poplar Forest.

Geometry

With Mr. Jefferson I conversed at length on the subject of architecture. . . .
He is a great advocate for light and air—as you predicted he was for giving you octagons.

—COLONEL ISAAC A. COLES TO JOHN HARTWELL COCKE, FEBRUARY 23, 1816

The design of the house at Poplar Forest is highly idealistic in its elegant geometry. Its exterior walls form a perfect, equal-sided octagon. Inside, the space is divided into four elongated octagons surrounding a central square. The simplicity of the floor plan displays Jefferson's attraction to the precision of mathematics.

The central space is a perfect cube, measuring twenty feet in all directions. With no exterior walls, it is lit from above: a sixteen-foot skylight streaks the room with exquisite light. This room also supplies an architectural surprise: a soaring two-story space in what appears, from the front, to be a single-story house. Perhaps most important, the entire Poplar Forest retreat, house and landscape, radiates out from this elegant central space.

Palladio

Since his death in 1580, the Italian architect Andrea Palladio (pictured below) has become one of the most influential designers of the Western world. The ancient Roman architect Vitruvius and the ancient classical ruins themselves were Palladio's source for understanding the principles of classical architecture. Palladio rigorously followed the rules of propriety, order, and proportion, but his designs also embodied a philosophy of humanism. This is especially evident in their harmonious relation to the rural landscape. Jefferson appreciated this aspect of Palladio, as he attempted to achieve his own close relationship of architecture and landscape.

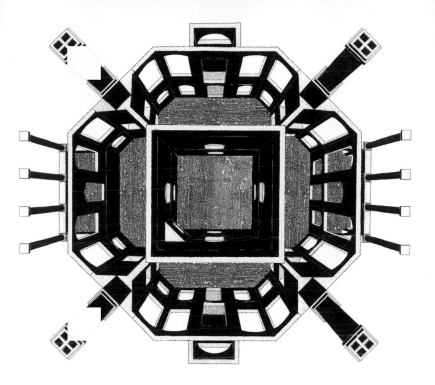

O C T A G O N S

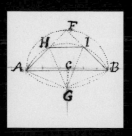

A drawing from Jefferson's notes labeled, "To draw 3 sides of an Octagon."

Among Jefferson's earliest architectural sketches, made when he was in his twenties, is a plan for a freestanding octagonal chapel. He based his design on Palladio's round Temple of Vesta, transforming it into an octagonal form using a prototype from an eighteenth-century British book. This represents an early example of Jefferson's lifelong tendency to create something original from two or more prototypes. He included octagonal and semioctagonal rooms in many of his designs.

Why this lifelong fascination? The geometry of octagons appealed to his mathematical mind. There was a practical reason too: octagonal rooms, studded with the large windows Jefferson preferred, create light-filled interior spaces. The residence at Poplar Forest was Jefferson's ultimate octagon: the only fully octagonal building he ever constructed and one of the first octagonal homes in America.

The cutaway view above reveals the house's geometric design: a perfect cube surrounded by four elongated octagons.

The central space is a perfect cube, dramatically lit by the skylight. The room also supplies an architectural surprise: a soaring two-story space in what appears, from the front, to be a single-story house.

Floor Plan

The north octagon holds the front passage and two small rooms, perhaps used for storage and occasionally as bedchambers. Jefferson stayed in the west bedchamber and his grandchildren usually stayed in the east chamber. The southern elongated octagon served as the parlor. Jefferson and his family used the central room for dining. It was the heart of the house, connected to the adjoining spaces by glass doors so that light and air flowed freely.

While the main floor comprised 1,927 square feet of living space, the equally large unfinished basement level was used for storage. Wine and cider were kept in the space directly below the dining room—its stone walls and a recessed floor maintained a cool temperature. Workers, free and enslaved, may have occasionally used the basement for accommodations.

Architectural Detail

In classical architecture, a building's or room's "order" determines the proportions and appearance of its columns, capitals, entablature, and decorative trim. For the exterior of the house at Poplar Forest, the two octagonal privies, and the bedchambers inside the house, Jefferson used the Tuscan order. Tuscan columns and capitals are plain. Likewise, the entablature, the wood trim that runs across the top of the columns, is decorated with simple moldings. This simplicity is meant to convey a sense of naturalness and integrity.

Adhering to the proper hierarchy, Jefferson used the Doric order in the central room—a more ornate decoration. For the room's entablature (in the interior, the trim that runs around the top of the room), he commissioned a sculptor to replicate an ancient frieze. The design, from the Roman Baths of Diocletian, alternated two elements: human faces, carved in low relief, and triglyphs, a "grill" of three vertical bars common to all Doric friezes.

Neoclassical architects carefully followed the Greek and Roman styles, which, Jefferson once wrote, "have had the approbation of thousands of years."

Construction of the Columns

Bricklayer Hugh Chisolm made the column shaft, base, and capital of molded brick. He then plastered over the brick with a lime mortar to achieve the appearance of stone. Because stone was scarce and expensive, Jefferson, following Palladio's example, used this technique at other building sites as well.

Conservators examining a few traces of the original lime mortar on the columns determined that it contained not only sand, lime, and fines (dirt), but also fired clay particles to achieve a suitable strength. The Poplar Forest restoration team was able to replicate the Jefferson-era lime mortar formula, which they applied in thin layers, closely duplicating the look of Jefferson's original columns.

■ Tuscan columns on the portico at Poplar Forest.

At Poplar Forest, however, Jefferson broke the rules, adding a third classical element, ox skulls, to the design. He explained to the confused sculptor, "You are right . . . those of the Baths of Diocletian are all human faces. . . . But in my middle room at Poplar Forest I mean to mix the faces and ox-sculls."

For the central room's entablature, Jefferson asked his sculptor to modify this ancient frieze.

In this private building, he felt he could follow his "fancy," which, he wrote, "I can indulge in my own case, altho in a public work I feel bound to follow authority strictly."

CORNICE

ENTABLATURE

FRIEZE

ARCHITRAVE

COLUMN CAPITAL

COLUMN SHAFT

For the parlor, Jefferson used the even more elegant Ionic order, commissioning his sculptor to replicate the entablature of the Roman temple of Fortuna Virilis. The delicate frieze consisted of small putti, or cherubs, alternating with ox skulls, connected by swags of foliage. Sadly, because of illness, Jefferson never saw this frieze in place.

Practical Concessions

For all his love of geometry and classicism, Jefferson yielded to practical concerns at Poplar Forest. In 1806, after construction of the house had just begun, he added two porches, two stair pavilions, and six doorways. Although they compromised his perfect octagon, it is easy to understand why Jefferson made these changes.

The front (north) porch—called a portico in the vocabulary of classical architecture—protected the entrance during bad weather and gave the house a neoclassical look. The rear (south) portico provided an ideal spot to view the lawn and countryside beyond.

Jefferson disliked staircases because he believed they wasted space. Without them, however, anyone walking between the upper and lower floors would have had to go outside. Even with the addition of internal stairs, anyone moving from the lower level to the main floor would have entered one of the bedchambers. Burwell Colbert, an enslaved man who served as Jefferson's principal waiter at Monticello, probably carried meals from the kitchen through the east bedroom to reach the dining room. The route taken between kitchen and table underscores the informality of Jefferson's retreat.

Where Were the Doors?

Restorers frequently must untangle webs of incomplete and contradictory evidence. In 1806, when Jefferson added porches and stairs, he also specified two new "doors of communication" on the main floor—but where? His request baffled restorers because the doorways did not appear on a floor plan drawn by one of Jefferson's workmen, John Neilson (who seems never to have visited Poplar Forest himself).

In fact, Neilson's floor plan appears to be inaccurate. Peeling back layers of the wall, architectural historians determined that Jefferson added the doorways between the small front chambers and the large bedchambers. To make matters more confusing, the doors had been bricked up in the mid–nineteenth century, and re-opened in the mid–twentieth century.

A Wing of Offices

The most significant alteration to the original design came in 1814. Planning for eventual year-round living at Poplar Forest, Jefferson added a one-hundred-foot-long wing of service rooms (he called them "offices") to make the house more practical. These rooms included an area probably used for storage, kitchen, cook's room/laundry, and smokehouse. Jefferson never ordered the construction of a corresponding wing on the west side.

The wing was tucked into the hillside so that only a low wall would have been visible from the front of the house. Its flat roof, called a terras roof, served a dual purpose: "About twilight of the evening,"

The floor-to-ceiling windows were among the French architectural details that Jefferson used in his own designs.

Jefferson noted, "we sally out with the owls & bats and take our evening exercise on the terras."

French Details

Jefferson adopted many aspects of the house's interior design from buildings he had seen in France. He especially liked the light-filled interiors there, and both the skylight in the dining room and the floor-to-ceiling windows in the parlor were French touches. Jefferson filled the south wall with triple-sash windows: when the bottom two portions are raised the window opening serves as a doorway to the porch. Jefferson often read in this south-facing room, which would have been flooded with light.

In each of the large bedchambers, Jefferson's workmen installed "alcove beds," which Jefferson felt saved space. An indoor privy—or toilet—was tucked away beneath the stairwell next to Jefferson's bedchamber, an unusual convenience for the time.

One important aspect of the exterior was also influenced by French architecture. Jefferson had observed that "all the new and good houses" in Paris were of a single story. He designed the house at Poplar Forest to be built into the crown of a hill, so that his two-story house would appear to be a single story from the front.

How Was Poplar Forest Built?

Jefferson chose to situate his house in a remote location because he wanted privacy, but this choice made the arduous early-nineteenth century building process even more difficult. He had to supervise

Fireplaces

In at least one case, design triumphed over practicality. Poplar Forest was outfitted with fifteen fireplaces constructed on the new theories of Count Rumford, the father of the modern fireplace. These were arranged ingeniously to use just four symmetrical chimneys. The fireplace in the central dining room ought to have had its own chimney, but this would have looked awkward and asymmetrical from the outside. Instead, Jefferson ran the flue diagonally through an adjacent wall to the northwest chimney. Unfortunately, this solution was the cause of two subsequent fires.

Jefferson had noted that "all the new and good houses" in Paris were of a single story. He built the house at Poplar Forest to appear that way from the front.

his work force from a distance, send materials from Monticello's workshop, and purchase building supplies in Lynchburg or have them shipped there. This proved to be a constant headache.

Construction began in the summer of 1806. After six years, Jefferson reported proudly, "Nothing will be wanting to finish it compleatly but the cornices and some of the doors." Nevertheless, three years after that he warned a friend, "You must come with your ears stuffed full of cotton to fortify them against the noise of hammers, saws, planes etc. which assail us in every direction." Finishing the house took twenty years (1806–1826).

When finished, it will be the best dwelling house in the state, except that of Monticello; perhaps preferable to that, as more proportioned to the faculties of a private citizen.

—THOMAS JEFFERSON TO JOHN WAYLES EPPES, SEPTEMBER 18, 1812

Bricks

We have burnt the bricks, and a finer kiln I never burnt in my life, it contains seventy-five thousand.

—HUGH CHISOLM TO THOMAS JEFFERSON, JULY 22, 1808

Hugh Chisolm, a "very good humored man" according to Jefferson, was his bricklayer. Chisolm, his brother, and several assistants made the bricks from a mixture of local clay and water, formed in molds, dried in the sun, and fired in kilns. Interior and exterior walls at Poplar Forest are made of brick, the lower level being sixteen inches thick and the upper level twelve inches thick.

Jefferson, then president of the United States, visited infrequently during the bricklaying phase. Without his supervision, some of the brick was poorly laid. There were structural problems as well: the stair pavilions were not bonded to the main wall of the house, and over time they settled, a problem only recently corrected by a modern restoration team.

John and Reuben Perry

Carpenters (and brothers) John and Reuben Perry installed much of the structural woodwork at Poplar Forest. Jefferson frequently had trouble getting Poplar Forest logs sawn at the local sawmill. Mill-sawn lumber requires a constant source of water, apparently not always available.

The modern restoration team faced the same problem, though for different reasons. Few modern mills will cut timbers longer than sixteen feet. The Perrys used massive beams. The oak timber over the columns on the portico, for example, is a twelve-by-twelve-inch beam that extends twenty-two feet in length.

Inside the house, among other tasks, John Perry laid the flooring, including the intricate herringbone pattern in the dining room. Jefferson's letter to Perry reveals both his understanding of carpentry and the kind of explicit instructions he sent his workmen: "The floor at Poplar Forest being intended for an under floor must be laid with oak. Poplar would not hold the nails, and pine is too distant & dear. All the floors of Europe are of oak. . . . Perhaps it may be easier done in herring bone. . . . In that case your sleepers should be but 14 I. from center to center, in order that the plank may be cut in two feet lengths." The European style oak

---

Laying the Foundation

I find by a letter from Chisolm that I shall have to proceed to Bedford. . . . I shall probably be kept there a week or ten days laying the foundation of the house, which he is not equal to himself.

—Thomas Jefferson to Martha Jefferson Randolph, June 16, 1806

Nine months into the job, Hugh Chisolm requested that the president of the United States come to Poplar Forest to help lay the house's foundation. Determining the correct angles and wall lengths for an octagonal house is a sophisticated mathematical calculation. Modern restorers have found a 2.5-degree shift in the foundation, which may indicate Jefferson's correction.

To form the forty-five-degree angles required in building an octagonal house, Chisolm had to mold special five-sided bricks (pictured below).

■ Carpenter John Perry used Jefferson's detailed instructions in laying the dining room's herringbone floor.

floors at Poplar Forest are one of the earliest examples in America.

John Hemmings

The most skilled craftsman to work at Jefferson's house was his slave John Hemmings. Over the course of ten years, Hemmings executed the fine decorative joinery work inside the house, such as doors, ornate Tuscan, Doric, and Ionic entablatures, and all of the neoclassical trim in the house. He also made the most ornate exterior details: Tuscan entablature, the classical balustrade, Chippendale-style Chinese rail, and louvered window blinds. Hemmings lived at Monticello, where he had received his training. He and the

During the first three years of construction, President Jefferson constantly corresponded with his hired and slave workers who were frequently working both at Poplar Forest and Monticello. These workers traveled back and forth with materials and tools.

For unexplained reasons, Jefferson seemed to only have one cart and one wagon that were shared between both places. "Jerry's wagon" was in constant use between the houses—moving crops, furniture, building materials, people, and tools.

In a letter written to his overseer at Monticello in July 1819, Jefferson described some of the tools needed at Poplar Forest: "It is so inconvenient for the house to spare the little mule and cart, and so few tools will be wanting here that they may bring them on their shoulders. They will need 2 hand saws, 2 jack planes, 2 pair chisels broad and narrow, some augers for common framing, a foot adze, and one of the narrow adzes which were made here to dig gutters in the joists. These things divided among three will weigh little."

members of his extended family made up the corps of domestic servants and artisans at Monticello. Hemmings' two nephews, Madison and Eston, were apprenticed to him and helped him repair the Poplar Forest house in 1825.

Hemmings could read and write and sent weekly reports to Jefferson from Poplar Forest. Describing cornices, architraves, and other details, he displayed a sophisticated knowledge of classical architecture.

Obtaining Materials

Poplar Forest's remote location made procuring materials difficult for Jefferson. His windows are a typical example. Jefferson insisted on oversized panes of "Hamburg or Bohemian glass of the middle thickness" which had to be ordered from Philadelphia and cut precisely because few workers in Virginia could trim glass.

After being delayed on the frozen Delaware River, the panes were sent to Washington, transferred to a ship in Alexandria, sailed to Richmond, and then poled upriver to Monticello. Typically half of any glass shipment was broken in this long journey, so Jefferson doubled his orders.

At Monticello, Richard Barry, a house painter and window glazer, inserted the panes into the sashes (which the carpenters at Monticello had made earlier). Ten months after the glass had been ordered, the completed windows were poled upriver to Lynchburg and carted to Poplar Forest.

Jefferson sometimes failed to find the materials he expected in Lynchburg. He

■ John Hemmings executed the most ornate exterior details, such as the roof's balustrade and Chinese rail.

was, perhaps, never more exasperated than in his efforts to finish plastering the house. After hiring a plasterer and instructing his overseer in every detail, including where to house the plasterer and what to feed him, Jefferson arrived at Poplar Forest to find the job had not even begun. Plaster of Paris could not be purchased in Lynchburg. The story ended happily when a neighbor, Charles Johnston, lent Jefferson five bushels. Still, the house was not fully plastered for another two years.

John Hemmings was a carpenter. He was a first-rate workman—a very extra workman. He could make anything that was wanted in woodwork.
—EDMUND BACON, 1860

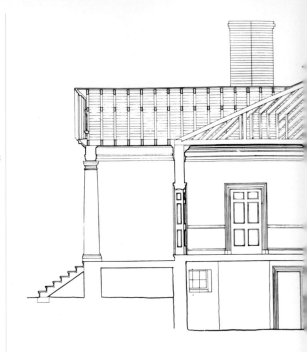

Bricklayer Hugh Chisolm's salary was recorded as twenty dollars a month. Jefferson paid all of his workmen but was sometimes late. Chisolm, for example, received final payment for making and laying brick at Poplar Forest more than two years after he had submitted the bill.

Many eighteenth-century construction workers traveled from job to job, living at their work sites. Chisolm at first stayed with the plantation overseer, Burgess Griffin. Loyal to his employer, he was outraged to learn that Griffin was charging Jefferson to lodge him. With a new straw mattress, he most likely moved to the barn.

Reuben Perry's Pay

Reuben Perry offered to trade his carpentry services for one of Jefferson's slaves, Jame Hubbard, Jr., who had run away from Monticello. Perry placed an ad in the Richmond newspaper to recover Hubbard, describing him as six feet tall, "stout limbs and strong made, of daring demeanor bold and harsh features, dark complexion." When Hubbard was caught, Perry subtracted $450 from his bill to Jefferson.

Repairs

About 3 o'clock there was greatest hail storm ever saw. Your house appears to have been in the center of it. The dammage is immense. . . . 77 panes of glass broken to atoms and the house is flooded with water.

—JOEL YANCEY TO
THOMAS JEFFERSON, JUNE 13, 1819

The house at Poplar Forest required constant repair and maintenance. During the hot summer of 1819, a catastrophic hailstorm with stones three inches in diameter destroyed the skylight in the central room. Jefferson wrote enthusiastically about his new design for

the room's flat roof. Consisting of a system of gutters, ridges, and shingles covered with a flat plank deck, he perfected the design at Monticello and would go on to use it for the wing of offices at Poplar Forest, and at the University of Virginia.

Making repairs to the rest of the roof after a small fire in 1825, Jefferson replaced the chestnut shingles with innovative new shingles, made of thin iron sheet metal dipped in tin. Iron sheet metal is no longer available, so the restorers came up with a compromise. Stainless steel, made in Georgia, was shipped to Connecticut to be hand-dipped in tin, then sent to New York state for cutting. Finally, the shingles were

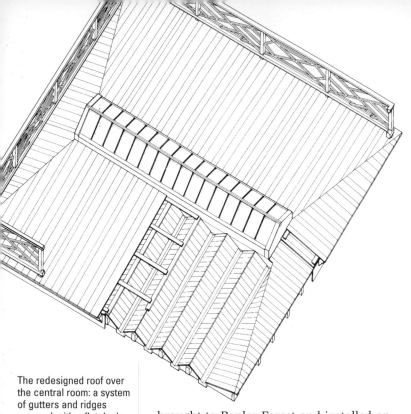

The redesigned roof over the central room: a system of gutters and ridges covered with a flat deck. The skylight runs down the center of the roof.

brought to Poplar Forest and installed on the roof. Countless letters attest to the fact that Jefferson's roof leaked, so a rubber membrane was installed under the shingles as a back-up system.

Jefferson appeared to enjoy the evolution of his house. However, its next owner, Jefferson's grandson Francis Eppes, felt differently.

Francis and his wife Mary Elizabeth moved to Poplar Forest after their marriage in 1823. On June 23, 1826, eleven days before Jefferson's death, the distressed Francis wrote his grandfather for help: the new tin-shingle roof leaked "not in one but a hundred places. . . . Large buckets of water pass through it." John Hemmings, in a rare mistake, had apparently installed the tin shingles in a manner contrary to Jefferson's instructions. The central room was the only dry place in the house.

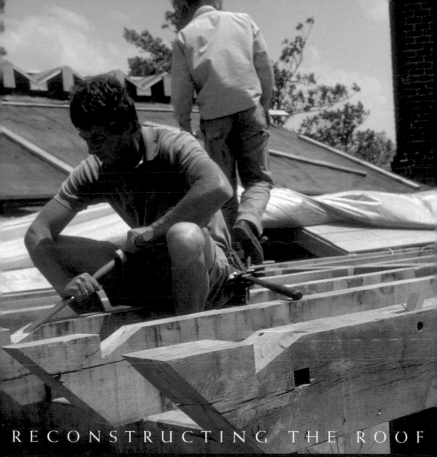

RECONSTRUCTING THE ROOF

■ **Restoration workers installing shingles on the new roof.**

Reconstructing the roof at Poplar Forest was one of the biggest challenges the restoration team faced. They built the entire terras—the flat roof around the skylight—by hand in the workshop using period techniques and special tools. Each piece was labeled and numbered, taken apart, then reassembled on the house. In one of the few modern concessions, restorers lined the roof, including the gutters and ridges, with a rubber membrane to prevent leaks.

The fully restored roof.

The two domed, octagonal privies that flank the mounds were correctly proportioned using Palladio's rules of architecture. Although mostly original, they now feature restored chestnut shingle roofs, lunette windows, and stairs.

THE LANDSCAPE

GARDENING AT POPLAR FOREST

O n a summer day in 1811, while visiting Poplar Forest, Jefferson wrote to a friend, "No occupation is so delightful to me as the culture of the earth, and no culture comparable to that of a garden. . . . Under a total want of demand except for our family table, I am still devoted to the garden, but tho an old man, I am but a young gardener."

Indeed, Jefferson's house at Poplar Forest once formed the center of an elegant geometric composition completed by the landscape. Most of this original landscape has vanished, and no Jefferson-era drawings of the grounds are known to exist, though his records provide some clues. Nevertheless, through extensive digging and lab analysis, archaeologists are developing a more complete picture of the gardens and grounds, so that eventually they may be restored.

Curtilage

I have engaged a workman to build offices, have laid off a handsome curtilage connecting the house with the Tomahawk, have inclosed and divided it into suitable appendages to a Dwelling house, and have begun its improvement by planting trees of use and ornament.

—THOMAS JEFFERSON TO JOHN WAYLES EPPES,
APRIL 18, 1813

In 1813, Jefferson established a sixty-one-acre enclosure, which he called his "curtilage." Beyond its boundary were the grounds of the working plantation. The area within contained a mixture of elements necessary to the villa retreat:

Garden Books

Jefferson's design for the ornamental grounds reflects his understanding of the era's garden fashions. He read influential books such as Robert Castell's *The Villas of the Ancients Illustrated* and the English translation of influential French gardener Dezallier d'Argenville's *La theorie et la pratique de jardinage.* One particularly important addition to his library was Thomas Whately's *Observations on Modern Gardening,* a text that Jefferson carried with him as he toured gardens in England with John Adams in the spring of 1786. While he dismissed many of that nation's great gardens as showing "too much art" or having "nothing remarkable," he later adopted selected elements in his grounds at Poplar Forest.

Jefferson also had a keen interest in plants, combining his scientific understanding of horticultural classifications from the work of Linnaeus with the practicalities of gardening gleaned from nurseryman Bernard McMahon's *American Gardener's Calendar* and Philip Miller's *Gardener's Dictionary.*

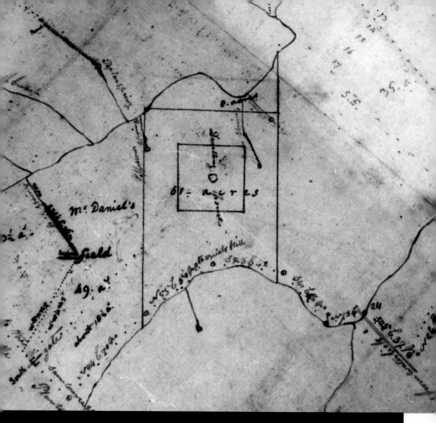

■ 1813 map of Poplar Forest shows curtilage between branches of the Tomahawk Creek.

kitchen gardens, ornamental plantings, orchards, and support buildings. At the heart of the curtilage, a circular road, "540 yds round" and lined on both sides with paper mulberry trees (pictured below), enclosed an area of approximately five acres. It was here that Jefferson carried out his inventive plan for the gardens at Poplar Forest.

Palladian Landscape

Jefferson's landscape design clearly expressed the Palladian idea that house and grounds should be joined into a seamless whole. He interpreted a five-part Palladian plan (perhaps from the Villa Barbaro): a central house, flanked by two wings, each

ending in a pavilion. However, Jefferson substituted landscape elements for bricks and mortar: double rows of paper mulberry trees formed the "wings" and earthen mounds replaced the pavilions.

Mounds were not an unusual feature in landscape design of the time, but Jefferson used them in an unusual way. In European gardens mounds provided elevated perches from which to view the surrounding landscape. Jefferson's mounds would have been closely planted with willow and aspen trees and later with shrubs, so they would not have functioned well as viewing points. Instead they formed part of the Palladian plan.

Beyond each mound was a privy, or outdoor toilet. These domed, octagonal little buildings were not only functional, they were also ornamental, adding another symmetrical element to the design. Indeed, they may have substituted for more elaborate garden temples common to great English gardens of the period.

Natural and Rational

The house, "wings," and mounds formed an east-west axis, separating the ornamental grounds into distinct areas which Jefferson designed to reflect two opposing sensibilities: on the north, or

The wings and pavilions of Palladio's Villa Barbaro (top) are made of bricks and mortar. At Poplar Forest (below), Jefferson used landscape elements instead.

Jefferson approached gardening like a scientist. In fact, he was honored at the 1792 meeting of the American Philosophical Society, where it was proclaimed: "In the various departments of this science, but especially in botany and in zoology, the information of this gentleman is equalled by that of few persons in the United-States." The twinleaf (pictured below), an American wildflower, was named *Jeffersonia diphylla* in Jefferson's honor.

In 1815 he received two overnight guests at Poplar Forest—a rarity—for a botany outing. Jefferson described Abbé Joseph Francis Correa de Serra as "a gentleman from Portugal, of the first order of science, being without exception the most learned man I have ever met with in any country" and Francis Walker Gilmer as "the best educated young man of our state." The trio spent several days "botanising" in the mountains and visited Natural Bridge. When Jefferson asked friends further south to host the two men, he warned, "At home in every science, botany is their favorite. As every plant of any singularity stops them, their progress is of course slow."

front of the house, he created a landscape that appeared natural, even wild. Jefferson had seen such gardens in England and wrote that their beauty "surpasses all the earth." On the south, the landscape was rational and geometric.

The North Entrance

Scientists have determined that the mature poplar trees still in front of the house today were twenty to thirty years old in 1806, when Jefferson began construction. Thus, visitors in Jefferson's day would likely have approached the house through a grove. Jefferson had advised a friend, "Under the beaming, constant & almost vertical sun of Virginia, shade is our Elysium. . . . Let your ground be covered with trees of the loftiest stature. Trim up their bodies . . . so that their tops shall still unite and yield dense shade."

Passing through the grove and rounding the carriage turnaround in front of the house, visitors would have encountered tree clumps and shrub beds. The clumps, planted at each corner of the house, contained "Athenian & Balsam poplars . . . locusts, common & Kentucky, redbuds, dogwoods, calycanthus, liriodendron." Though carefully chosen to look attractive together, the trees and shrubs would have been densely planted, appearing to be a wild thicket.

Archaeologists have investigated one of three oval beds. Located northwest of the house, it contained prickly locust, a shrub with bright pink blossoms. Other beds in front of the house contained roses of various sizes.

Several Jefferson-era tulip poplars stand among the trees in front of the house today.

This landscape style, mimicking the natural world, was then the most modern approach. It harmonized with the north façade of the house—which was also modern, as single-story houses were in vogue in late-eighteenth century Paris.

The South Lawn

If you would engage the negroes to dig and remove the earth South of the house, 90 feet wide, down to a foot below the lower floor, and descending from thence due south 1 inch in every 10 ft.

—THOMAS JEFFERSON TO HUGH CHISOLM, JUNE 5, 1807

The sunken lawn was originally rectangular. After adding the wing of offices to the east side of the house, Jefferson instructed his workers to alter the east bank so that it angled away from the house, underscoring the symbiotic relationship between house and landscape. This altered plan was temporarily re-created on the south lawn in 1999 with potted shrubs.

Behind the house, Jefferson envisioned a more ordered setting: a carefully

delineated lawn with rolling fields beyond. Controlled, geometric, and open, it was the opposite of the shady grove in front of the house.

This landscape was dominated by a large sunken lawn that Jefferson originally envisioned as a rectangle, ninety feet wide and more than two hundred feet long. Phil Hubbard, possibly with the aid of other enslaved men and women, undertook the Herculean task of

creating this artificial space, moving more than 36,000 cubic feet of soil by shovel and wheelbarrow across the hillside to build the earthen mounds flanking the house.

Here landscape and architecture combined to express a classical sensibility: the south façade of the house, where both stories are clearly displayed, includes a Roman-style arcade (hiding the lower-level entrance) topped by a classical portico, reflecting Jefferson's look back to ancient times.

Archaeological Discoveries

Archaeologists were surprised to discover two sets of planting holes along the sunken lawn's east bank: the earlier

Gardening and Friendship

In the late eighteenth and early nineteenth centuries, gardening was a social activity. The elite, in both Europe and America, toured gardens, traded plants, and shared insights about the art and science of gardening.

While at Poplar Forest Jefferson shared gardening advice—and a variety of plants—with his neighbors. His friend Charles Clay provided European mulberry trees (pictured below) to complete Jefferson's planting scheme between the house and mounds. Jefferson reciprocated the following year by sending paper mulberries to Clay, noting that "they are charming near a porch for densely shading it." He also provided his neighbor with vegetables including salsafia, a root that when "fried in batter it can scarcely be distinguished from a fried oyster."

Many of the ornamentals that graced the Poplar Forest grounds traveled from afar. Once on the property, many plants resided for a time in the nursery, a space adjacent to the stables that Jefferson designated for young trees and shrubs. Here were laid out cuttings of weeping willow alongside saplings of Athenian and Lombardy poplars, aspens, and paper mulberries. One wagonload arrived from Monticello with the instructions that "the branches of plants without roots are to be cut into lengths of 5 or 6 buds each and stuck into the ground 2 or 3 buds deep to take root." Over time, the gardener used these rooted saplings to create new plantings or supplement older ones. The Gelder rose was one of the shrubs Jefferson planted along the banks of his sunken lawn.

Martha Randolph packaged sets of tulips, hyacinths, and other "blooming roots" from the gardens of Monticello one fall and sent them to be planted at her father's retreat. Jefferson's "famous" Hudson strawberries arrived at Poplar Forest via Philadelphia.

holes ran in a straight line, forming the edge of the original rectangular lawn. However, a later set of planting holes angled away from the house. On the west bank, archaeologists discovered only the straight line of holes. Had Jefferson designed an asymmetrical lawn? Alterations to the east bank apparently followed construction of the "wing of offices," which replaced the original rows of trees on the eastern side of the house. That Jefferson changed the landscape in relation to the architecture underscores their symbiotic relationship.

He may have planned a similar restructuring to the west but never implemented the change. A sunken lawn with both banks angling away from the house would have created an optical illusion: from the house, the distant landscape would have appeared closer. From the end of the lawn, the house would appear more distant. Jefferson used this technique, called "forced perspective," on the design of the lawn at the University of Virginia.

Plantings for the Sunken Lawn

In 1812, Jefferson directed, "Plant on each bank, right & left, on the S. side of the house, a row of lilacs, Althaeas, Gelder roses, Roses, calycanthus." Research has revealed that this experienced gardener made his choices thoughtfully. All of these shrubs were hardy and grew well in clay soil. They also had similar growth rates so the visual balance of the landscape would be maintained as they grew. Each shrub bloomed at a different time of year, providing seven months of color and scent, from early spring to September.

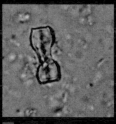

A Phytolith as seen through a microscope.

Archaeologists are extracting tiny bits of evidence from the soil to determine what Poplar Forest's landscape looked like over time.

The soil contains seeds, pollen, and phytoliths — the silica "skeletons" of plants. Differences in the size and shape of these remains tell

scientists what plants they came from.

In one project, archaeologists collected soil from the sunken south lawn. Scientists examined the microscopic botanical evidence extracted from these samples. They found pollen grains from ornamental shrubs and flowers — including althaea and viburnum — that Jefferson mentioned in his planting instructions. Because insects carried these pollens, the grains remained close to where the plants had been, confirming their use and location in the garden. Recovered phytoliths included European grasses from the cultivated turf in the center of the lawn, and native grasses and weeds on the banks.

Wood charcoal also provides evidence, suggesting what type of wood enslaved workers burned for fuel. Differences in wood charcoal over time reflect ongoing forest clearance and the regrowth of fields.

Botanical remains can also tell more than just landscape stories. Seeds from the slave quarters indicate what foods people received as provisions or grew and gathered for themselves.

Archaeologists continue to study botanical evidence to help develop an accurate interpretation of gardens and farm fields.

■ Jefferson's granddaughters remembered that sometimes the grounds at Poplar Forest looked wild and desolate.

The Vegetable Garden

Jefferson noted many vegetables in his garden correspondence. Among them was the tennis-ball lettuce, pictured below.

For Jefferson, the vegetable garden provided the "cheapest, pleasantest & most wholesome part of comfortable living." The garden at Poplar Forest was eighty yards square and enclosed by a seven-foot high picket fence "so close that a hare cannot get into it." Jefferson's enslaved gardener Nace planted many vegetables including tennis-ball lettuce, tomatoes, beans, squash, artichokes, spinach, asparagus, and Jefferson's favorite, peas. Nace also planted fruit trees and raspberry and

gooseberry bushes. He probably planted and tended the ornamental grounds as well.

Reality Intrudes

As in all things, Jefferson was an idealistic gardener, and he may not have executed all of his plans for Poplar Forest. The landscape also changed over time: he replanted areas where certain species seem to have died out and made design adjustments as the house itself evolved.

Jefferson's long absences meant the gardens suffered, and his vision of the landscape was often at odds with what he saw when he arrived. Perhaps this is why he appreciated the forgiving nature of the landscape, where he found "such a variety of subjects, some are always coming to perfection, the failure of one thing repaired by the success of another."

Archaeologists excavate the south lawn.

Jefferson and his granddaughters spent the hours before bedtime reading together in the parlor.

Th: Jefferson salutes mr Vest r̄
and respect and there being no p
Monticello to see to the weekly trans
mails to this place, he asks the favor y
to do him that kind office, sending wee
bury mail all _letters_, the _Enquirers_, ar
directed to him, and to retain all ot
pamphlets, books, or other prackets, t
hears from him again.
Poplar Forest Nov. 29. 20.

D A I L Y   L I F E

JEFFERSON, FAMILY, AND FRIENDS AT POPLAR FOREST

With his house only half complete, Jefferson began regular visits to his new retreat in 1809. He was sixty-six years old, in good health, and recently retired from the presidency. For the next fourteen years, he made the trip three to four times a year, in all seasons, staying from two weeks to two months. Jefferson was frequently occupied with managing his plantation, gardening, and supervising house and landscape construction. He also pursued his many intellectual interests. To the modern person, Jefferson's leisure activities may not seem very relaxing:

> I have amused myself with calculating the hour lines of an horizontal disk for the latitude of this place, which I find to be 37 22' 26''. The calculations are for every 5 minutes of time and are always exact to within less than half a second of a degree.
>
> —THOMAS JEFFERSON TO CHARLES CLAY, AUGUST 20, 1811

> I amused myself with reading seriously Plato's Republic. I am wrong however in calling it amusement, for it was the heaviest task-work I ever went through.
>
> —THOMAS JEFFERSON TO JOHN ADAMS, JULY 5, 1814

> I shall be engaged in Bedford in making a geometrical measurement of the Peaks of Otter which has never been done yet, altho deemed the highest mountains of our Ranges.
>
> —THOMAS JEFFERSON TO JOSEPH MILLIGAN, OCTOBER 27, 1815

At Poplar Forest he found in a pleasant home, rest, leisure, power to carry on his favorite pursuits—to think, to study, to read.

—ELLEN WAYLES RANDOLPH COOLIDGE TO HENRY S. RANDALL, 1856

Notes on the State of Virginia

Though acclaimed for his elegant writing, Jefferson published only one book, *Notes on the State of Virginia*, largely written at Poplar Forest in the summer of 1781. The book was written in response to a request from Monsieur de Marbois of the French legation in Philadelphia. Marbois sought statistical information on several states, including Virginia, for his government. Jefferson's resulting study was greatly esteemed in his own day, earning him a reputation as a scholar. Readers today still find it rewarding.

While providing a vivid description of eighteenth-century Virginia, the book also reveals a great deal about Jefferson's mind. Curious about an enormous range of subjects, he sought out detailed facts and figures on Virginia's population, industry, geography, and social and political life. His romantic sensibility is also evident in rapturous descriptions of Virginia's natural wonders, including several of his favorite sites near Poplar Forest. He called Natural Bridge "the most sublime of nature's works" and estimated the nearby Peaks of Otter to be the highest mountains in North America.

At other times he made architectural plans, surveyed his property, corresponded about the "progress and prospects" of the University of Virginia, made a list of mountains "in order in which they are seen from Poplar Forest, beginning in the S.W. and proceeding N. Eastwardly," and advised a local tavern-keeper on the best French wines to purchase.

Reading and Writing

I have fixed myself comfortably, keep some books here, bring others occasionally, am in the solitude of a hermit, and quite at leisure to attend to my absent friends.
—THOMAS JEFFERSON TO BENJAMIN RUSH, AUGUST 17, 1811

In nearly every letter he wrote at Poplar Forest, Jefferson mentioned reading. Eventually, his library grew to nearly seven hundred volumes, twice the number of books found in most upper-class homes of the period. These were in addition to his large collection at Monticello.

Some of the books at Poplar Forest were "petit-format" editions, meaning they were small in size, allowing Jefferson to maintain a portable library away from home. (He had begun the collection while living in Washington.) Among the petit-format authors were Virgil, Tacitus, Caesar, Cicero, Ovid, Horace, Aesop, and Homer, authors Jefferson read not in English translation, but in their original languages.

The Poplar Forest library contained many other books, including 108 volumes of British poets, 25 volumes of Italian

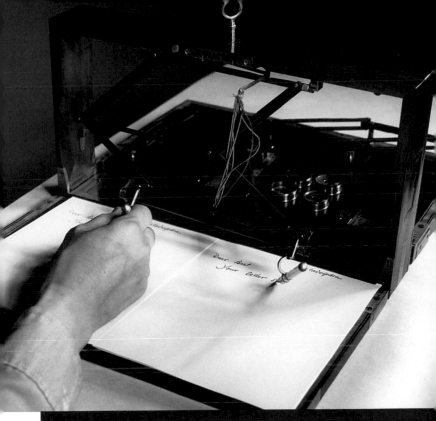

■ Visitors to Poplar Forest today can use a replica of Jefferson's polygraph in the hands-on history area.

poets, 38 volumes of Shakespeare, a 52-volume series of Buffon's *Histoire Naturelle*, and Jefferson's own *Notes on the State of Virginia*. No wonder his granddaughter Cornelia complained, "Tomorrow sister Ellen & myself have to put numbers on all of grandpapas books & it will take us nearly the whole day which I am very sorry for."

Jefferson wrote almost 20,000 letters in his lifetime, corresponding with friends and family, but also with admiring strangers curious to

Jefferson used this polygraph machine to copy letters.

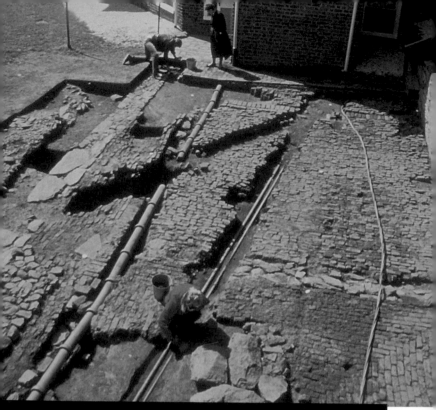

Jefferson probably added the wing of service rooms (being excavated here) to make the house more comfortable for his grandson, Francis Eppes, who eventually inherited the property.

know more about him. Using a machine called a polygraph at both Poplar Forest and Monticello, he made a copy of every letter. He called it "the finest invention of the present age." The polygraph at Poplar Forest had been a gift from the inventor, John Isaac Hawkins.

Family

Jefferson's happy marriage to Martha Wayles Skelton had lasted ten short years, and only two of their six children survived to adulthood. He did find domestic happiness in his later years, however. His eldest daughter, Martha Jefferson Randolph, had eleven children and the younger daughter, Maria Jefferson

Eppes, had one surviving son. Jefferson had hoped his descendants would settle in Bedford. Though this was not to be, many of them fondly remembered time spent there with Grandpapa.

Ellen and Cornelia Randolph

> *[He] will pay his Spring visit to Bedford this month. Cornelia is going certainly but they had not decided which of the remaining three will accompany him, as each puts in her claim.*
>
> —ELIZABETH TRIST TO NICHOLAS P. TRIST,
> APRIL 5, 1821

In 1816 Jefferson began bringing his grandchildren to Poplar Forest. Of Martha Jefferson Randolph's eleven children, Jeff, Virginia, Mary, Septimia, and James all visited. But it was Ellen and Cornelia who spent the most time there. Ellen was twenty years old and Cornelia seventeen when they first came to Poplar Forest, and their thoughtful, charming, and sometimes gossipy letters provide an intimate glimpse of life at Jefferson's retreat.

Jefferson called the girls "the severest students I have ever met with," because they spent so much time reading. Schooled from a reading list developed by their grandfather and well-educated mother, they read history, literature, philosophy, and classics in several languages. Ellen recalled reading Latin for seven to eight hours a day, six weeks at a stretch.

I consider all my grandchildren as if they were my children, and want nothing but for them.

—THOMAS JEFFERSON TO JOHN WAYLES EPPES, APRIL 30, 1816

A terra-cotta bust of Jefferson's granddaughter Cornelia Randolph.

■ Jefferson's granddaughter Cornelia sometimes sketched beneath the central room's skylight.

The girls also did needlework and longed for a piano for fear that their musical skills would decline. When the damaged dining room skylight had to be boarded up, Cornelia dutifully pursued her drawing in the dark, producing a picture of a dog with its nose "in so unseemly a place," that, her sister Ellen wrote, "it shocks me to look at it."

Jefferson expected proper conduct and hard work from his granddaughters, but he also wanted them to have fun. One of their most exciting excursions was to Natural Bridge, a trip "attended with disasters and accidents" that the two young women would never forget. After nearly killing themselves trying to cross a rotting bridge,

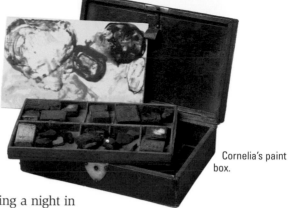

Cornelia's paint box.

they had lunch with several local men, one with "savage" looks, and the other with his "hairy breast exposed." Spending a night in Greenlee's tavern, Jefferson did not mind sharing his room with strangers (the custom of the day). The girls, however, were so disturbed by the dirty sheets that they slept on top of them.

The beauty of Natural Bridge made up for the challenging journey. And their humorous letters hint that they enjoyed the eye-opening experience of meeting people so different from themselves. Certainly their grandfather was at ease with everything—and everyone—they encountered.

Maintaining the House

Monticello, full of guests and grandchildren, required a large crew of cooks, waiters, maids, and other domestic servants. At Poplar Forest, just a few enslaved women worked in the house when Jefferson was in residence. Hannah, the stepdaughter of headman James Hubbard, cooked and washed. Maria helped make the house ready for habitation and Edy or Aggy cleaned and assisted part of the day during Jefferson's visits. Burwell Colbert and Israel Gillette Jefferson served as Jefferson's personal servants, and traveled with him from Monticello.

Natural Bridge

Jefferson wrote in *Notes on the State of Virginia* that Natural Bridge was "so beautiful an arch, so elevated, so light: and springing as it were up to heaven, the rapture of the spectator is really indescribable."

In fact, in 1774 he purchased the bridge and a 157-acre tract surrounding it. He often thought of building "a little hermitage" at the site. Despite his financial troubles, he wrote in 1815 that he would never sell the land: "I view it in some degree as a public trust, and would on no consideration permit the bridge to be injured, defaced or masked from public view." Natural Bridge was sold in 1833 as part of Jefferson's estate.

Jefferson would have interacted closely with these slaves. Few records of how owner or slave felt about the other exist. However, when Burwell became seriously ill one summer, Jefferson's granddaughters sent detailed letters to Monticello expressing their concern. Cornelia wrote that they woke in "terror every morning" that he had died during the night. Ellen frankly admitted, "Grandpapa Cornelia and myself make as complete a tribe of ignoramuses as I do know, and I do not believe our three heads combined contain as much medical knowledge as would save a sparrow." The local doctor was called in, but it was another slave, John Hemmings, who apparently nursed Burwell to his recovery. Ellen recorded, "Johnny is one of my favorites and more so, now than ever since I have witnessed his kind attentions to Burwell."

Social Life

The story of the neighborhood immediately was that I had brought a crowd of workmen to get ready my house in a hurry for Bonaparte. Were there such people only as the believers in this, patriotism would be a ridiculous passion.
—THOMAS JEFFERSON TO MARTHA JEFFERSON RANDOLPH, AUGUST 31, 1815

The rumor that Napoleon Bonaparte, recently defeated at Waterloo, was coming to Poplar Forest astonished Jefferson. In fact, his social life there was informal. Ellen described his relationship with his neighbors: "It was pleasant to see him in company with the country gentlemen of the neighborhood, they treated him with so much affectionate and respectful

Hannah

One of Jefferson's enslaved servants, Hannah, was born at Monticello in 1770 and moved to Poplar Forest with her family as a teenager. There she married Solomon, whose fate is unknown. She later married Hall, a blacksmith and hog-keeper. Hannah worked in the fields and served as Jefferson's housekeeper, cooking and washing for him. Hannah had five children, the last born in 1812, when she was forty-two years old.

In 1818, Hannah wrote Thomas Jefferson a letter when she learned that he was too ill to visit. She wished him well and professed her Christian faith.

Master I write you a few lines to let you
know that your house and furniture are all saf
u would be glad to know ... I heard that ...
... pect to come up this fall I was sorry
... was so unwell you could not come th ...
... any time but I hope as you have been so blessed
... at you considered it was god that done it
... we all ought to be thankful for what
... us we ought ... serve and ...
... you ma ...

frankness—were so much at their ease
with him, whilst they held him in such
high honor. Their wives too were as
happy as queens to receive him."

Two of his closest neighborhood friends
were the Reverend Charles Clay, whom
Jefferson had known years before in
Albemarle County, and James Steptoe, a
friend from the College of William &
Mary. Jefferson occasionally shared
"plantation fare" with these men. When
Clay sent Jefferson a "mess" of asparagus,
he invited himself to dinner with a note
proposing to find out "how you have it
dressed." Jefferson's granddaughters were
sometimes critical of the country folk they
met in Bedford. When Reverend and Mrs.

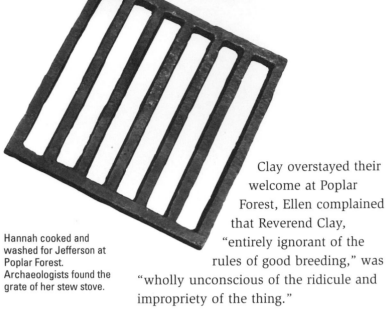

Hannah cooked and washed for Jefferson at Poplar Forest. Archaeologists found the grate of her stew stove.

Clay overstayed their welcome at Poplar Forest, Ellen complained that Reverend Clay, "entirely ignorant of the rules of good breeding," was "wholly unconscious of the ridicule and impropriety of the thing."

Jefferson's only public, formal social occasion came in 1815 in Lynchburg, the result of a chance encounter which Jefferson described in a letter, "I was most agreeably surprised to find that the party whom I thought to be merely curious visitants were General Jackson and his suite, who passing on to Lynchburg did me the favor to call."

General Andrew Jackson, hero of the War of 1812, was on his way to Washington to answer trumped-up charges that he had mistreated civil authorities during the war. Cities along the way held celebrations for him, and the one in Lynchburg was first-rate. It included a parade at which, the Richmond *Enquirer* reported, "Thomas Jefferson, Esq. the great supporter of our republican institutions, added dignity to the procession." Jefferson both gave and received toasts at the dinner for 300 guests held at Martin's, the area's largest tobacco warehouse. While Jackson stayed

THE TYPICAL DAY

Jefferson's granddaughter Ellen, a frequent visitor to Poplar Forest, described Jefferson's daily schedule:

We met in the morning for an early breakfast, which, like all his other meals, he took leisurely. Whilst sipping his coffee or tea he talked with us, and if there was anything unusual to be done, arranged our plans for the day. The forenoon, whilst we followed our own desires, he passed in the drawing room with his books. With the exception of an occasional visitor, he was seldom interrupted until the hour of his ride. We dined about three, and as he liked to sit over his wine (he never took more than three glasses, and these after, and not during dinner), I always remained at table till he rose. His conversation at this time was particularly pleasant—easy, flowing, and full of anecdote. After dinner he again retired for some hours, and later in the afternoon walked with us on the terrace, conversing in the same delightful manner, being sometimes animated, and sometimes earnest. We did not leave him again til bed-time, but gave him his tea, and brought out our books or work. He would take his book from which he would occasionally look up to make a remark, to question us about what we were reading, or perhaps to read aloud to us from his own book, some passage which had struck him, and of which he wished to give us the benefit. About ten o'clock he rose to go, when we kissed him with warm, loving, grateful hearts, and went to our rest blessing God for such a friend.

—Ellen Wayles Randolph Coolidge to Henry S. Randall, 1856

late in the evening to dance with the
ladies, Jefferson, who disliked dancing,
returned home.

During his years at Poplar Forest, the
nearby community of Lynchburg became,
"the 2nd town in the state for business,
and thriving with a rapidity exceeding
anything we have ever seen," according to
Jefferson. At the same time, the family's
social engagements in the nearby counties
of Bedford and Campbell increased. In
1819, Cornelia complained that they would
soon have "more trouble & vexation on
account of company than we ever had at
Monticello." Hosting more formal dinners,
with ladies in attendance, was a challenge

at the country retreat, where supplies could be scarce. One evening, Cornelia noted with mortification, they would be forced to serve "such bread for dinner as we utterly disdained this morning, no one even tried to eat it."

Food

As a working plantation, Poplar Forest produced most of its own food. Jefferson himself preferred to eat vegetables with meat as a "condiment" and oversaw a large garden. Cattle, hogs, and sheep were also raised on the plantation.

To supplement what was produced on site, Jefferson used an agent in Richmond, who shipped requested items to another

Weary Days and Wasted Hours

Like their grandfather, Ellen and Cornelia used Poplar Forest as a retreat. Ellen expressed their frustration when social obligations intruded upon their study time one summer:

For the last three days the carriage has been ordered as regularly as the breakfast. . . . Our plans of industry are much disconcerted by all this—& I have never found my time pass so unpleasantly . . . after the heat and trial of dressing, we leave home, at a time of day when the thermometer is perhaps 95 degrees in a little confined carriage which has got so thoroughly heated standing a few moments before the door, that it is like entering the mouth of an oven, & after a ride of four five or six miles over a rough dusty road under a broiling sun, we arrive fatigued, flushed and dirty, sit up four or five hours in company, silent and uncomfortable, too much exhausted to enjoy society even if it were of the best kind, and return home in the evening to mourn over the weary day and wasted hours. This sort of life seems however to agree with us both—I have never seen Cornelia look better or handsomer.

—Ellen Wayles Randolph to Martha Jefferson Randolph, August 11, 1819

agent in Lynchburg. Planning a long stay with Ellen and Cornelia, Jefferson once requested "a keg of tongues & sounds, a small keg of crackers, a small box of raisins, and a good cheese . . . add a barrel of shad." Sounds, the air bladders of fish, were considered a delicacy.

Jefferson also purchased food locally, often from his slaves. On one two-month visit in 1819 he bought forty-four chickens and six ducks. Not having an icehouse, they frequently borrowed ice from a neighbor, Mr. Radford. Ellen complained, "Grandpapa insisted on our using that cooler (refrigerator, I believe he calls it) which wasted our small stock of ice, and gave us butter that ran about the plate so that we could scarcely catch it, and wine about blood heat."

Ellen and Cornelia were understandably grateful to a neighbor, Mrs. Walker, who sent "a tidy mulatto girl, with an apron as white as snow" with gifts of food: fruit, melons, apples, ripe peaches, vegetables, cake, and sweetmeats.

Furnishings

Tell Johnny Hemings to finish off immediately the frame for the round table for this place that it may come by the waggon. . .
–THOMAS JEFFERSON TO WILLIAM BACON
DECEMBER 5, 1811

At Poplar Forest, Jefferson wrote, he had only "the strictly necessary." In 1809 he purchased three dozen "stick" or Windsor chairs, painted black "with yellow rings." Cornelia's drawing shows what the chairs would have looked like.

YOUTHFUL RECOLLECTIONS

One of Jefferson's early biographers, Henry Randall, asked Ellen (pictured above) to describe her visits to Poplar Forest. Her recollections attest to her close relationship with her grandfather.

His young grand-daughters were there to enliven it for him, to make his tea, preside over his dinner table, accompany him in his walks, in his occasional drives, and be with him at the time he most enjoyed society, from tea till bed time. . . . My grandfather was very happy during these sojourns in a comparatively simple and secluded district—far from noise and news—of

both of which he got too much at Monticello; and we, his grand-daughters, were very happy too. It was a pleasant change for us, a variety in life and manners. We saw, too, more of our dear grandfather at those times than at any other. . . . He interested himself in all we did, thought, or read. He would talk to us about his own youth and early friends, and tell us stories of former days. He seemed really to take as much pleasure in these conversations with us, as if we had been older and wiser people. Such was the influence of his affectionate, cheerful temper, that his grandchildren were as much at their ease with him, as if

they had not loved and honored and revered him more than any other earthly being. I . . . not only listened with intense interest to all he said, but answered with perfect freedom, told my own opinions and impressions, gave him my own view of things, asked questions, made remarks, and, in short, felt as free and as happy as if I had been with companions of my own age.

—Ellen Wayles Randolph Coolidge to Henry Randall, 1856

Next to the chair in her drawing is a table with a revolving top, made by Jefferson's slave John Hemmings, a skilled carpenter and joiner.

Jefferson was partial to dumbwaiters and he had two at Poplar Forest, made of walnut and pine. These little tables were used in the dining room: a servant, most likely Burwell, would have placed food on the shelves then left the room, allowing family and guests to serve themselves.

Tantalizing descriptions of other furnishings exist. According to an 1815 tax record, the house contained at least eleven pieces of mahogany furniture and an Englishman visiting in 1816 described "large mirrors" that betokened Jefferson's "French taste." Perhaps most intriguing, one granddaughter recalled opening a package from Monticello containing a "head of Christ" which everyone found "ingenious." What it was exactly, we may never know.

Travel

We always stopped at the same simple country inns, where the country-people were as much pleased to see the "Squire," as they always called Mr. Jefferson, as they could have been to meet their own best friends.
—ELLEN WAYLES RANDOLPH COOLIDGE TO HENRY S. RANDALL, 1856

Using an odometer attached to his carriage, Jefferson measured the distance between Monticello and Poplar Forest at exactly ninety-three miles. The trip, inevitably described as wearying, took an average of three days, enlivened only slightly by the odometer, which rang a bell at regular intervals.

Jefferson designed his carriage himself and had it constructed at Monticello. It was drawn by four horses. Jefferson's servant Burwell usually followed on a fifth horse, preceding a mule-drawn cart carrying baggage and supplies. After leaving Monticello, the entourage

Jefferson's Siesta Chair

In the summer of 1819, Jefferson, now seventy-six years old, suffered a violent arthritis attack while at Poplar Forest. He sent a request to his daughter Martha, "While too weak to set up the whole day, and afraid to increase the weakness by lying down, I longed for a Siesta chair which would have admitted the medium position." Also called a "campeachy" chair because its frame was made of a type of mahogany found in Campeche, Mexico, these recliners were the current fad among Jefferson's circle of Virginia friends.

He had several different styles of Campeachy chairs (one of which is pictured below). The one sent to Poplar Forest had a melon-shaped crest rail with inlaid stars and was covered in "red marocco" leather.

■ On average, it took Jefferson three days to travel the ninety-three-mile journey from Monticello to Poplar Forest.

usually spent the first night at Warren, the home of Jefferson's close friend Wilson Cary Nicholas. They then crossed the James River by ferry, stopping for meals and lodgings at taverns, which the girls described as sometimes pleasant, sometimes dirty.

Jefferson's grandchildren clearly enjoyed their trips to Poplar Forest. Even the journey, as Virginia described, provided special private time with their grandfather, who treated them with care and affection: "Early in the morning, he was sure to have some additional wrapping to put over the shoulders of each of us. . . . His cheerful conversation,

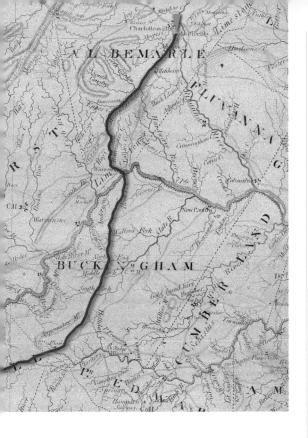

so agreeable and instructive, his singing as we journeyed along, made the time pass pleasantly. . . Our cold dinner was always put up by his own hands; a pleasant spot by the road-side chosen to eat it, and he was the carver and helped us to our cold fowl and ham, and mixed the wine and water to drink with it."

Case bottles, like the ones pictured here, were used to carry beverages and other liquids between Monticello and Poplar Forest.

The pediment was missing from the south portico for more than 150 years before its restoration reestablished the portico's proper look.

■ Jefferson's enslaved workers farmed the rolling fields surrounding the house at Poplar Forest.

THE PLANTATION

WORK AND SLAVERY
AT POPLAR FOREST

S oon after he inherited the Poplar Forest property from his father-in-law, Jefferson made an entry in his farm book listing twenty-seven names: Guinea Will, Betty, Hall, John, Davy . . . These were some of the slaves now living and working on the plantation.

Jefferson extolled the virtues of the agrarian life. He considered farming to be his profession and the tobacco and wheat grown at Poplar Forest (he ranked Bedford County as the "finest part of Virginia" in terms of soil and climate) supplied him with a significant portion of his income. His ideal of the citizen-farmer, however, stands in stark contrast with the reality that enslaved men and women worked his land. These people, who had lived at Poplar Forest long before Jefferson built his house, are integral to its story.

Farms

Jefferson managed his vast estate in Bedford using a traditional Virginia plantation system. He divided the land into separate farms, each with a different overseer, work force, dwelling houses, and farm buildings. By the time Jefferson resided at Poplar Forest, there were two active farms, Tomahawk and Bear Creek.

Enslaved Workers

Seven extended families lived on the plantation and worked the farms. Slaves worked from sunup to sundown, from nine hours a day in the winter to fourteen hours in the summer. They worked six days a week, with Sundays and Christmas off.

The Enslaved Community Over Time

When Jefferson inherited Poplar Forest in 1773, only one family and a few unmarried individuals were living there. Before the 1790s, there was a great deal of flux within the community, as people were sold, given away through marriage, and moved to and from Monticello. By the mid-1790s, the community became more stable with a slow, natural increase in population. By the end of Jefferson's life, ninety-four people lived in slavery at Poplar Forest, more than half of them children. The community was broken up in the years just prior to and following Jefferson's death, when people were sold to pay his debts or passed down to Francis Eppes, his grandson who inherited the house and 1,074 acres of land.

The slave community living at Poplar Forest during Jefferson's lifetime was a mix of older people who may have had direct connections to West or Central Africa and others whose families had been in America for several generations. This was a formative period for African American culture, as people maintained ties to their heritage and created new ways to deal with the world around them.

At age sixteen young men and women were assigned long-term jobs. Those who performed domestic work cooked, washed laundry, cleaned house, served food, attended horses in the stable, gardened, cut wood, and hauled water. Farm work included clearing land, plowing, sowing seeds, harvesting, threshing, making roads, building fences and outbuildings, and managing livestock. Some workers learned specialized crafts such as blacksmithing, coopering, basket- and shoemaking, spinning, weaving, carpentry, joinery, and bricklaying. Slaves also ran errands and carted goods to market.

Ten-year-old children watched over younger siblings. Twelve- and thirteen-year-olds helped their parents in the field or were sent to Monticello to learn a skill. Most enslaved men and women worked until death. Bess, at age sixty-four, continued to make butter and spin wool.

Overseers

For a salary of about $200 per year, a share of the crop, and a cabin, Jefferson's overseers managed the work force and the day-to-day farm operations.

Jefferson himself, intimate with every aspect of the plantation, was clearly in charge. He provided overseers with instructions for planting, harvesting, and selling crops. He knew each slave who worked for him and shared his thoughts about their skills and work habits. He even made decisions about housing, food rations, and blanket and clothing allowances, carefully writing out instructions for the overseers to implement.

aired.

nings. 35. &07
nings. 70.
our 59.
n 93.
t. 99. Dec.
61.
9.
87. run away
apr. 02.
3

Negroes in Bedford
July 1805.
Jame Hubbard
Cate. ab. 1749.
armistead. 71.
Nace. 73.
Sarah. 88. aug.
Nancy 91. Sep. Oct.
Rachael. Oct. 73.
Borrel. 94. & 180
Cate. 97. aug.
Joe. 1801.
Lania. 1805

Maria. 76.
Nace of aug

JAMES HUBBARD, SR.

The life span of James Hubbard, Sr., called Jame, roughly coincided with Jefferson's own. Born in 1743, Hubbard became Jefferson's property at age thirty. He is listed above in a memo Jefferson sent to his overseer.

For several years, he lived at Monticello and worked as a waterman, carrying goods to market in Richmond and returning to Monticello with supplies. Jefferson clearly trusted him, as he was loosely supervised and may have visited friends and family on his trips.

Hubbard was a foster father to three young children whose parents had died. He married Cate, already a mother to two girls. Together they had six more children. When Jefferson moved Jame and his family to Poplar Forest, he became the headman, overseeing field laborers. He had his own cabin and received double rations.

Hubbard's children had a range of experiences: Nace and Hannah became Jefferson's trusted headman and housekeeper; Nancy died as a teenager; Joan was given away as part of Martha Jefferson's dowry; the younger Jame attempted to run away several times and was sold.

Jefferson considered tobacco, pictured here, "infinitely wretched" because it depleted the soil.

Many of Jefferson's overseers seem to have been ineffective. He once blamed his financial problems on "4 years of Goodman and Darnell," referring to two of them. He eventually sought to solve his farm management problems by hiring Joel Yancey to oversee the overseers. When he ended his long tenure as superintendent, Yancey thanked Jefferson for his "friendship and politeness" as an employer.

Jefferson perceived himself as the protector of his "people" (as he called his slaves). He loathed physical violence. Nevertheless, he sometimes instructed overseers to use the whip: when Jame Hubbard, Jr., repeatedly ran away from Monticello, Jefferson had him severely flogged in front of his friends and coworkers.

Headmen

Jefferson used the term "headmen" to refer to slaves who supervised groups of field laborers on the plantation. Jame Hubbard, Sr., and Nace served Jefferson as headmen at Poplar Forest. Jame Hubbard oversaw Bear Creek farm for many years; two maps note the location of "Hubbard's field." Jefferson described Nace as "the former headman, and the best we have ever known."

Headmen lived in a "world between," fulfilling the demands of their owners while living in a community of relatives and friends whom they supervised. There is no evidence that enslaved people aspired to be headmen. Headmen typically received better rations and housing for their services, but in playing the role of taskmaster, disciplinarian, and informer, they may have paid a price.

Crops

Tobacco and wheat were the cash crops. Jefferson considered tobacco "infinitely wretched" because it depleted the soil and provided no food for the farmer or his work force. Getting tobacco to market took eighteen months of hard labor. Poor weather, economic instability, or mishandling could quickly eliminate a season's profits. Wheat, Jefferson argued, was "the reverse in every circumstance." It preserved the soil's fertility and fed the laborers.

Self-Sufficiency

In addition to cash crops, the field workers had to produce enough food to

I know that neither people nor horses can work unless well fed, nor can hogs or sheep be raised.
—THOMAS JEFFERSON TO JEREMIAH GOODMAN, DECEMBER 23, 1814

Progressive Farming

I think it the duty of farmers who are wealthier than others to give those less so the benefit of any improvements they can introduce, gratis; & I shall have more pleasure in seeing this benefit spread over the country & being instrumental to it, than all the Dollars would give me.

—Thomas Jefferson to Joseph Dougherty, June 27, 1810

Jefferson was a progressive farmer, always interested in new crops and machinery. Soil conservation was a particular passion. In 1811, writing from Poplar Forest, he described his crop rotations to his friend and fellow farmer, Charles Willson Peale, "Our rotations are corn, wheat & clover, or corn, wheat, clover and clover, or wheat, corn, wheat, clover and clover, preceding the clover by a plaistering, but some instead of clover,

continued on facing page.

serve Jefferson's family and the large plantation community. Many crops—corn, pumpkins, potatoes, oats, and barley, for example—were grown primarily for internal purposes. Butter, milk, meat, grains, peaches, and other fruits produced in Bedford supplied people living at both Poplar Forest and Monticello.

Livestock, including hogs, cattle, and sheep, were also raised for internal consumption. Jefferson explained to his overseer how the hogs should be apportioned within the plantation: "Supposing there are 40. bacon hogs at this place & 32 at Bear creek reserve 23. for the negroes, which allows a hog apiece for Hal & Jame Hubbard, and half a one for every grown & working negro, keep 6. for my use & Chisolm's then take out the Overseer's parts and send the rest to Monticello."

The men often fattened the livestock at Poplar Forest, then drove them to Monticello for butchering. In 1814, on the day after Christmas, Davy, Bartlet, Nace, and Eve began the ninety-mile journey. Jefferson instructed his overseer, "Caution them against whipping the hogs. The last year there was one so bruised all over that not a single piece of it could be used."

The more efficient plow that Jefferson designed.

■ Laborers are depicted in the field in this mid-nineteenth century sketch, by Edwin Forbes of a Virginia wheat harvest.

Weaving and Spinning

Jefferson established spinning and weaving operations so that women could make clothes from hemp, flax, and wool produced on the plantation. For many years, this work was done in the slave quarters. By 1814, there was a spinning house at Poplar Forest.

Older women taught their daughters, granddaughters, and nieces—usually at age twelve or thirteen—the craft of spinning using a spinning wheel and later a spinning jenny. Lucy and Sally worked with Bess and Abby, while Nisy and Maria learned from Cate. Maria and Sally journeyed to Monticello to learn the craft. Maria apparently became "a capital

substitute mere rest." Clover, when planted in rotation with tobacco and wheat, restored the soil's fertility. Gypsum plaster served as Jefferson's fertilizer.

Jefferson was zealous about the need for farmers to share innovative ideas, improved crops, and new machinery. He invented a more efficient plow (pictured at left) but never patented his design so that other farmers could freely benefit from the idea.

Debt

When Jefferson inherited Poplar Forest from his father-in-law, he also inherited a staggering debt. He sold other land, but hesitated to sell too much as he felt it was "the only sure provision" for his children. In general he avoided selling enslaved workers "as long as there remains any prospect of paying my debts with their labour," adding, "In this I am governed solely by views to their happiness."

Jefferson was frequently disappointed in the sales of his crops. Many years, he was able to pay only the interest and no principal on his debts. He then extended his credit, entering into a never-ending cycle.

Among the artifacts found in the area of the slave dwellings were these scissors and thimbles.

spinner," but of Sally, Jefferson wrote, "we can make nothing at all. I never saw so hopeless a subject. She seems neither to have the inclination nor the understanding to learn."

When fabric imports were restricted during the War of 1812, spinning operations took on greater urgency, as Jefferson noted, "We have no chance therefore of clothing the negroes next winter but with what we shall make ourselves." Scissors, straight pins, and thimbles found in the slave quarter indicate that women sewed for themselves and their families.

Other Work

Besides working in the fields and gardens, men and women were involved in cottage industry. Blacksmiths made and repaired tools, wagon parts, horseshoes, and worked in the field when they had no work in the shop. Jefferson also set up a coopering shop to make the barrels needed for storing tobacco and wheat and shipping them to market.

The Wagon

Though ninety miles apart, the work at Poplar Forest and Monticello—agriculture, house construction, and industry—was linked. Wagons and carts carried goods back and forth between the two

■ A "ghost structure" erected at Poplar Forest shows the dimensions and location of a duplex slave structure that housed two families.

plantations for twenty years. On one occasion, for example, Dick brought pork, butter, peaches, and lard to Monticello, and returned with doors, wine, and books for Poplar Forest. On another occasion, Jefferson noted that Dick was missing a bushel of dried peaches, fifteen pounds of soap, and half a basket of apples, writing, "These repeated accidents cannot but excite suspicions of him, sufficient to make us attentive in the future."

Jefferson wrote explicit instructions about what the wagon should carry and anxiously implored his overseers to get it moving from one site to another. Slaves and workers often walked to save wagon space for food and materials.

Jefferson recorded names, birth dates, and family affiliations of his slaves, made notes about blankets and food rations, and corresponded with his overseers about their work. He did not, however, say much about their private lives. Archaeologists have begun to discover where the slaves lived, what they ate, and the types of objects they owned and used in daily life.

In analyzing their finds, archaeologists at Poplar Forest wondered, what choices could Jefferson's slaves have made? How did they define themselves? Indeed, slaves at Poplar Forest—and throughout Virginia—appear to have had some control over what they wore, what they ate, and with whom they lived. Some slaves earned small amounts of money, which they used to improve their standards of living.

Income

Jefferson paid enslaved workers for working on their own time or for doing especially unpleasant tasks. In seeking labor to dig out the south lawn, he wrote, "I would gladly pay them for it. But it is only with their own free will and undertaking to do it in their own time. The digging and removing is worth a bit a cubic yard." Phil Hubbard dug for a year or longer.

The joiner John Hemmings received $20 per year as a "gratuity," the equivalent of one month's wages for a white carpenter or joiner. Jefferson's personal servant, Burwell Colbert, who often accompanied him to Poplar Forest, received the same annual encouragement.

Throughout the Southeast, enslaved families raised poultry and tended their own vegetable gardens. During visits to Poplar Forest, Jefferson recorded purchasing chickens, ducks, turkeys, and eggs from several women. During times of inflation these women were able to charge Jefferson hefty prices.

Resistance

Resistance took subtle forms in the slave community, including feigning illness, breaking tools, stealing, and slowing work. Slaves also ran away.

Jefferson's friend, Elizabeth Trist, described one case of physical assault. Billy "attacked the overseer—knocked him down and wounded him in several places with a knife." Jefferson's house servant and Billy's mother, Hannah, apparently stopped the bleeding "by holding the wounds together till they sent for a

Doctor." Though his face was "horribly mutilated," the overseer recovered. Trist finished, "They say that he was by no means a hard task master."

Another friend of Jefferson's reported the outcome of the trial held in Bedford, "Billy was found guilty of stabbing & was sentenced to be burnt in the hand and whipped." Jefferson sent him and three others he suspected were connected with the crime—Hercules, Gawen, and Manuel—to Louisiana to be sold.

Enslaved Families

Though marriages between enslaved men and women were not legally recognized, Jefferson honored them to promote stable family life within the plantation community. When an overseer refused to let a newly married couple live together, Jefferson intervened, arranging for the couple's house. As he once explained, "a child raised every 2. years is of more profit than the crop of the best laboring man." His promotion of family stability only concerned married couples and young children. Teenagers were often sent off the property to learn a craft or could be leased or sold.

Women who married within the plantation received a bed and a cooking pot from Jefferson. The women at Poplar Forest bore eight children on average, their first between the ages of eighteen and twenty. Poplar Forest men usually became fathers at the age of twenty-five.

Maria having now a child, I promised her a house to be built this winter. Be so good as to have it done.
—THOMAS JEFFERSON TO JOEL YANCEY, NOVEMBER 10, 1818

Coins found in a slave quarter at Poplar Forest.

Nearly all who lost a spouse remarried.

Not everyone married within the plantation. When families resided on separate plantations, the children typically lived with their mothers. Fathers would visit on Sundays or holidays. The communities at Poplar Forest and Monticello were especially intertwined. When people journeyed between the plantations to visit and for work assignments, they saw friends and relatives who lived on other plantations along the way, resulting in a wide network of connections.

Slaves lived in log cabins clustered in fields and work areas. Archaeologists

■ An artist's rendering of what some of the slave dwellings at Poplar Forest probably looked like.

have found evidence of several slave dwellings east of Jefferson's house. The largest cabin was 15 x 25 feet. It was probably built of logs and functioned as a duplex. A single fireplace heated each room, with chimneys built of wood and lined with clay for fireproofing. Jefferson noted that it took three workers six days to build such cabins.

Personal Belongings

In each side of the large duplex at Poplar Forest, archaeologists discovered a pit or root cellar had been dug beneath the floor. Some archaeologists believe that the cellars were used to store food and valuable personal belongings in cabins

Stone pipes, found in a slave quarter at Poplar Forest, were probably made by Jefferson's slaves.

that offered little privacy. Indeed, one cellar at Poplar Forest appears to have contained clothing, tools, and iron hardware. Archaeologists also found locks and keys, which were probably used to guard valuable belongings.

Other archaeologists believe people used root cellars to hide stolen goods. John Hemmings seemed to describe such a situation when he told Jefferson that "Nace takes every thing out of the garden and carries them to his cabin and burys them in the ground. . . . The people tells me that he makes market of them at the first opportunity."

Personal Time

The cabin sites discovered at Poplar Forest faced away from the overseer's house, presumably to allow some privacy. A fence enclosed the yard, extending the living quarters. Slaves probably spent much of their personal time in these yards, where they cooked, washed laundry, planted gardens, and worshiped. They also gathered there to socialize, drink, and talk. Archaeological evidence shows that someone was making stone pipes at the site and probably used free time to gather stone and work it.

Some traveled off the plantation to visit family and attend church. Slaves also shopped with the little money they earned. Local records show that Will, from Poplar Forest, purchased rum, buttons, thread, and cloth from a New London store in 1772.

Reading and Writing

A few individuals within the enslaved community at Poplar Forest could read and write, and archaeologists found a portion of a writing slate in the quarter. Jefferson did not forbid them from learning as some owners did. On the contrary, he corresponded regularly with John Hemmings about construction at Poplar Forest. Hannah, Jefferson's house servant, could also read and write.

Fragments of ceramics found around the slave dwellings at Poplar Forest.

■ Enslaved people living at Poplar Forest likely purchased these buttons and other items of personal adornment at local stores.

Clothing

People received winter and summer sets of clothing, shoes, and stockings. Their clothing rations, woven from "coarse" cloth, were undoubtedly plain and uniform.

Archaeologists found clothing accessories in the quarter—buttons, some of them silver-plated, glass beads, and part of a gilded necklace. Advertisements for runaways, which described clothing in detail, confirmed that these items of adornment—which must have provided an important form of self-expression— were indeed popular.

Food and Medicine

Jefferson recorded giving individuals rations, which included salted fish, corn, wheat, salt, and whiskey. For meat, they supplemented rations of pork with poultry they raised themselves and game: archaeology in the quarter revealed evidence of opossum, rabbit, white-tailed deer, and squirrel. They tended their own vegetable gardens and foraged in the surrounding landscape for edible weeds and wild fruits.

Carbonized remains of herbs such as pokeweed, smartweed, and bedstraw were also found in the quarter. Folk healers probably used such plants to prepare teas for the sick. Jefferson's neighbor, Dr. William Steptoe, sometimes treated enslaved people for serious illness, but it was probably quite common for them to rely on healers from within their own community before turning to a doctor. There appears to have been some sort of hospital, as Jefferson refers to a "house for the sick" on the property.

A high infant mortality rate at Poplar Forest led Jefferson to suspect that enslaved mothers were not able to care for their sick children properly, so he encouraged overseers to allow them to do so.

Slaves could also use health as a form of resistance, sometimes feigning illness to avoid work. Those too ill to work in the fields did light work indoors, such as making shoes and baskets.

Jefferson's Attitudes about Slavery

The whole commerce between master and slave is a perpetual exercise of the most boisterous passions, the most unremitting despotism on the one part, and degrading submissions on the other.

—THOMAS JEFFERSON, NOTES ON THE STATE OF VIRGINIA, 1782

How could the man who wrote "all men are created equal" own more than two hundred human beings?

Although Jefferson grew up with slavery—when he was born in 1743, it had existed in Virginia for nearly seventy-five years—he was clearly troubled by it, once calling it a "moral and political depravity." Throughout his life he wrote about the issue, expressing contradictory views and attitudes that changed over time. As a young Virginia legislator, he pushed to allow private citizens to free their enslaved people but was ultimately unsuccessful. His original draft of the Declaration of Independence included language opposing the transatlantic slave trade.

Jefferson remained tied to the system partially out of his own economic self-interest. He may have mediated the contradictions by taking a strong paternal attitude toward his enslaved workers. He considered them part of an extended family for whom he was responsible. He also sold people, used corporal punishment, and broke up families. He freed John Hemmings, Burwell Colbert, and several other people from Monticello but did not free anyone who resided primarily at Poplar Forest.

Thomas Jefferson on Slavery

What a stupendous, what an incomprehensible machine is man! Who can endure . . . imprisonment or death itself in vindication of his own liberty . . . and inflict on his fellow men a bondage, one hour of which is fraught with more misery than ages of that which he rose in rebellion to oppose.

—Thomas Jefferson to Jean Nicolas De Meunier, June 26, 1786

No body wishes more than I do to see such proofs as you exhibit, that nature has given our black brethren, talents equal to those of other colours of men, & that the appearance of a want of them is owing merely to the degraded condition of their existence.

—Thomas Jefferson to Benjamin Banneker, August 30, 1791

There is nothing I would not sacrifice to a practicable plan of abolishing every vestige of this moral and political depravity.

—Thomas Jefferson to Thomas Cooper, September 10, 1814

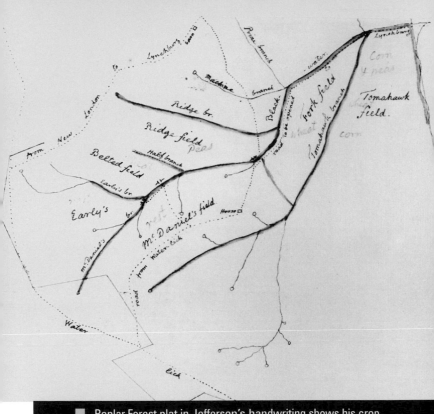

Poplar Forest plat in Jefferson's handwriting shows his crop rotation and fields under cultivation by his slaves. Although undated the paper bears the watermark 1809.

Jefferson eloquently articulated the highest ideals of human equality. He is a symbol for democracy throughout the world. Yet Jefferson owned slaves his entire life. For many, he has become a symbol of America's struggles with racial inequality, his successes and failures a mirror of the nation's own.

Archaeologists search for clues about daily life at Poplar Forest.

While Jefferson viewed Poplar Forest as a retreat, the public is invited to visit today.

AFTER JEFFERSON

OTHER FAMILIES AT POPLAR FOREST

I give to my grandson Francis Eppes, son of my dear deceased daughter Mary Eppes, in fee simple . . . part of my lands at Poplar Forest. . . . I subject all my other property to the payment of my debts.

—THOMAS JEFFERSON'S WILL, DATED MARCH 16, 1826

Shortly after his daughter Maria died in 1804, Thomas Jefferson wrote to his son-in-law, John Wayles Eppes, with a broken heart, "While I live, both of the children will be to me the dearest of all pledges." Only Maria's first child, three-year-old Francis, survived to receive his grandfather's attentions, and Jefferson eventually took charge of his education. As a teenager, Francis visited Poplar Forest frequently during breaks from the New London Academy, located just three miles away. Francis moved to Poplar Forest with his wife of less than a year, Mary Elizabeth (known as Elizabeth), in 1823, three years before Jefferson's death.

Jefferson made what proved to be his last visit to Poplar Forest to help Francis and Elizabeth settle in, because, as he explained, "beginnings are always difficult with young H-keepers." He was eighty years old. His daughter Martha and granddaughters Virginia and Cornelia came along. Always an indulgent grandfather, Jefferson sent the girls on a shopping trip with a note to the merchant, "Should anything strike their fancy in your assortment be so good as to let them have it on my account."

Jefferson's Death

Thomas Jefferson died on July 4, 1826, fifty years to the day from the signing of the Declaration of Independence. For his family, his death was "a calamity of frightful magnitude."

The Poplar Forest land and slaves Jefferson inherited from his father-in-law, John Wayles, had come with a large debt. Virginia agriculture suffered from years of embargo and war and Jefferson earned only a small salary in public office. In 1819, his financial future was doomed: $20,000 in notes which he had reluctantly endorsed for his friend Wilson Cary Nicholas, with whom he visited on his journeys to and from Poplar Forest, came due. Jefferson's daughter, Martha, and her children deeply mourned his loss and were also faced with paying the huge debt.

Elizabeth Eppes reflected that Jefferson's family had experienced "uninterrupted peace, tranquility, and pleasure" when he was alive. "I have ever felt cheered and enlivened by . . . the God-like benevolence and tranquility which shone in Mr. Jefferson's countenance and voice and manner," she wrote. "But alas that happiness has now fled. Those days are gone forever."

The house at Poplar Forest was remodeled after a fire in 1845. In the central room, the ceiling was lowered and the trim altered.

Thomas Jefferson died in 1826, and Francis inherited the house and 1,074 acres of the plantation. The rest was sold to help pay Jefferson's debts. Soon afterward, Francis became frustrated with life in Virginia, where tobacco had depleted the soil and bad weather made farming difficult. Facing financial ruin, Francis wrote to a cousin, "Damn the crop say I, and the State to boot." Elizabeth Eppes explained, "These gullied worn out fields, and this unfinished leaking hull of a house, have become more than ever distasteful. . . . Tobacco is the only thing which can be made here,

Jefferson's grandson Francis Eppes lived at Poplar Forest from 1823 to 1828 with his wife.

and after vast labour and expense, in raising and manufacturing the vile weed . . . to find still that no profit must be expected, is disheartening indeed."

Though the estate had been appraised at well over $20,000, Francis was anxious to move and took less than $5,000 for it. In 1828, after five years at Poplar Forest, he and Elizabeth moved to Florida. Elizabeth died in 1835 and Francis later remarried. Francis Eppes (pictured below left) became a successful farmer and pillar of the community, serving as mayor of Tallahassee and one of the trustees of the school that became Florida State University.

A Campbell County neighbor, William Cobbs, bought the property from Francis. After Cobbs's daughter Emma married Edward Sixtus Hutter in 1840, they lived there as well. In the years just prior to and following Jefferson's death, most of the slaves were sold or given to Francis. By the time the property was sold, the slave community who had worked Jefferson's plantation was dispersed, and other enslaved people were situated on the land.

Cobbs-Hutter

We regret to hear that the dwelling-house of Wm. Cobbs Esq. of "Poplar Forest," in Bedford, about seven miles from Lynchburg, (extensively known as the former residence of Ex. President Jefferson, by whom the building was erected,) was burnt to the ground on Friday last. The disaster was occasioned by sparks falling on the roof from the chimney which had taken fire.

–*LYNCHBURG VIRGINIAN*, NOVEMBER 24, 1845

■ William Cobbs and Edward Sixtus Hutter repaired the house after the 1845 fire. They made changes to the landscape including removing and replacing trees and shrubs. Fields, woodlands, and other elements of the larger farm also saw changes.

An 1845 fire damaged the house at Poplar Forest so badly that reports

Christian Sixtus Hutter, one of the ten children Edward Sixtus Hutter raised at Poplar Forest, eventually inherited the house, which he owned from 1889-1946.

described it as destroyed. In fact, though much was lost, Jefferson's brick construction saved the house itself. When William Cobbs and his son-in-law Edward Sixtus Hutter made repairs, they also remodeled the house for year-round residence. As a growing family they needed a practical farmhouse, not a classical villa retreat.

Most significantly, Cobbs and Hutter lowered the ceiling of Jefferson's central room from twenty to twelve feet high, eliminated the skylight, and installed new

rooms above. With this, the shape of the roof changed, and dormer windows were added for light. A staircase in the cube room provided access to the upper and lower areas, so that the family could reach all floors without going through a bedroom. They adapted the lower level for dining, bedrooms, and a kitchen.

The family also bricked up six windows, two doorways, and a fireplace on the main floor. Their new trim reflected the current style, known as Greek Revival, characterized by a very plain look. The alcove beds were removed and Jefferson's bedroom was divided into two rooms. They also tore down the deteriorating wing and built dependencies separate

■ The nonprofit Corporation for Jefferson's Poplar Forest has completely restored the exterior of the house.

from the house. Of these, two brick tenant houses and a barn survive. Jefferson's landscape was dramatically altered.

With this redesign, the harmony of Poplar Forest was lost—the classical detail and relationship of parts to the whole were no longer apparent. The ornamental landscape had become a farm. Though architectural historians would disagree, one Hutter relative described the changes as "valuable improvements." They did, at least, underscore the very personal nature of Jefferson's retreat. It had proved completely unsuitable for all the subsequent owners.

Later Owners

The Hutter family owned the property for 118 years until 1946, when James O. Watts, Jr., a Lynchburg attorney, purchased it and began to operate a dairy farm. He also reintroduced sheep to Poplar Forest. He renewed some of the house's original features, reopening windows and installing parlor trim that resembled Jefferson's. At the same time, he further modernized the house, adding additional bathrooms and electricity, for example.

Reserving fifty acres surrounding the house, the Watts sold off parcels, and modern subdivisions sprang up on every side. In 1980, Dr. James A. Johnson, a North Carolina doctor, bought the property. Three years later it was for sale again. Unoccupied, the house began to deteriorate. Prospective buyers contemplated adapting it as a restaurant or for other uses that would have permanently destroyed historic features. Local preservationists, encouraged by Dr. Johnson, attempted to organize a rescue effort but were daunted by the cost.

The Rescue

In 1984, a small group of local residents took on the awesome challenge of launching a rescue attempt. With one gift as down payment, the nonprofit Corporation for Jefferson's Poplar Forest took title to Dr. Johnson's fifty acres and bought an adjacent tract back from developers who were about to build another subdivision on what was left of the farmland. With support from many people, Poplar Forest opened to the public on July 4, 1986.

When restored to its pristine state . . . it will constitute . . . a treasure for the nation.

—A. L. ROWSE, EMERITUS FELLOW, ALL SOULS COLLEGE, OXFORD UNIVERSITY

Stabilization and Research

Despite changes over the years, several features of Jefferson's retreat design were readily identifiable, including three buildings, a portion of the circular road, the sunken lawn, the poplar trees, and the mounds.

After stabilizing the house with concrete footings, architects, architectural historians, and craftsmen spent six years painstakingly examining every inch. Peeling away layers of plaster and wood trim installed after Jefferson's time, they reached Jefferson's brick and mortar, where they discovered ghost marks—indications of original architectural details. Finally, they drew up plans to restore Poplar Forest authentically, consulting approximately 1,500 Jefferson letters relating to the plantation.

Restoration

Re-creating early nineteenth-century techniques and processes has given us great insights. By doing the work in the same manner, we have had many more unforeseen questions and challenges, but we have learned a lot about the reality of constructing something like this. In a sense, we are repeating history.

—TRAVIS McDONALD, DIRECTOR OF ARCHITECTURAL RESTORATION, POPLAR FOREST

The brickwork reveals not only Jefferson's technology but also the idiosyncrasies of the individual bricklayers.

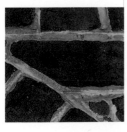

The approach to restoration at Poplar Forest is unique. Instead of focusing merely on the end result, contemporary masons and carpenters are using the same building methods Jefferson's craftsmen used, and visitors can watch them at work. The exterior of the main

house has been completely restored. The wing of offices to the east is undergoing reconstruction. Craftsmen returned Jefferson's cube room to its original dimensions of 20'x 20'x 20' and reconstructed the sixteen-foot, thirty-two-pane skylight, the largest one Jefferson ever designed for a residence.

The restoration team has learned a great deal about the challenges that Hugh Chisolm, John and Reuben Perry, and John Hemmings faced. They are using custom-made, hand-molded reproduction bricks and authentically re-created mortar. The carpenters have replicated the mortise-and-tenon roof construction and the tongue-and-groove white oak floors.

L I M E   P U T T Y

Much of what the craftsmen in Jefferson's time knew wasn't shared. That was part of the art and mystery of their trade. I've been trying to unlock that mystery.
—James Price, Poplar Forest mason

The authentic restoration process at Poplar Forest takes considerably more time and effort than simply substituting modern building methods. For example, Hugh Chisolm did not leave a formula for his lime putty, a key mortar ingredient. To replicate it, staff used laboratory analysis and a source Jefferson would have used, the ancient Roman architect Vitruvius. They also went through much trial and error.

The masons built their own lime kiln with walls four feet thick, burning many cords of wood to produce sufficient heat to calcine off (the process of burning off the carbon dioxide) the limestone into quicklime.

The best quicklime is then "slaked" into putty by pouring water over the stone, causing a boiling process to begin, crumbling and melting the quicklime. The slaked lime is hand-sieved and run into aging pits to mature until ready to be used.

After several efforts, the modern masons reproduced the Jefferson-era putty, which is used for mortar, as well as plaster and lime wash, in the restoration process.

This authentic approach to restoration has earned Poplar Forest great professional recognition and the National Trust for Historic Preservation's prestigious "Honor Award." Visitors will continue to have a unique educational opportunity as they watch what is essentially a Jefferson-era construction project in progress.

Archaeology

Archaeological evidence provides an alternative view of the past. By finding the things that people threw away, and the houses and yards they abandoned, we can learn about their lives free from the intentional biases that creep into documents, and discover information that they never thought important enough to record.

—BARBARA HEATH, DIRECTOR OF
ARCHAEOLOGY AND LANDSCAPES,
POPLAR FOREST

Archaeology is ongoing at Poplar Forest. Why? Jefferson's notes and correspondence present an incomplete picture. Many of the elements of the Poplar Forest landscape are referenced in letters, but no documents record their exact locations. Besides location, archaeology can provide information about the materials used in buildings, how long they stood, and what went on within them, as well as the arrangement and longevity of plants in the grounds. Even when documents do exist, Jefferson's designs were not always executed as planned, and some decisions were changed on-site. Archaeology can also provide clues to challenge or flesh out the "official" record. This is especially true when studying slavery, where the perspectives of the enslaved are often absent from the documents.

Among the artifacts that have been recovered from the site is this bone-handled fork, dyed green to simulate the look of jade.

Excavation of the Wing of Offices and Kitchen Yard

Historians knew little about Jefferson's wing of offices before excavations began. Archaeologists discovered that the wing had four principal rooms: what appears to be a possible storage room, kitchen, cook's room/laundry, and smokehouse. They uncovered the original brick floors, stone hearths, and wall foundations. From the thousands of artifacts associated with these spaces, they learned much about how the rooms functioned when Jefferson was alive and how their use changed over time.

In the course of excavations, it became clear that Jefferson was incorrect when he

■ An archaeologist digging in the wing of offices discovered the cast iron grate of a "stew stove" in the cook's room.

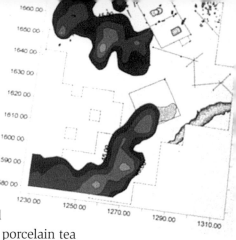

wrote in a letter that the wing was 110 feet long. John Hemmings recorded the correct length of 100 feet.

Individual artifacts found during the wing excavations also provided new information about life at Poplar Forest. A fork with a bone handle, dyed green to imitate jade, Chinese porcelain tea and coffee wares, and English transfer-printed plates provided new information that Jefferson enjoyed the latest styles while dining at Poplar Forest. Animal bones discarded outside the kitchen even indicate what was served for dinner.

Archaeologists create maps to examine the variation and concentration of different types of artifacts at an excavation site.

Though Jefferson described the food at Poplar Forest as "simple plantation fare," archaeologists found the cast iron grill of a "stew stove" in the kitchen. Such stoves allowed the cook to control temperatures more precisely than with an open hearth and indicate that Jefferson's food was probably more sophisticated than he described.

Archaeologists also found fragments of a bell and pieces of a system that once connected the dining room of the main house to the wing, so Jefferson and his family could summon Hannah, Burwell, or the other slaves working in the wing. Tools related to sewing, shoemaking, and other crafts indicate the tasks that occupied the people living in the wing when not cooking, cleaning, and waiting on Jefferson and his family.

Restoring a historic house using traditional methods requires craftsmen with specialized skills and materials imported from throughout the world.

Without enough Jefferson-period brick to raise the dining room walls back to the original twenty-foot height, hand-molded restoration brick was produced at a special facility in North Carolina. Blacksmiths in Colonial Williamsburg made the wrought-iron nails needed for roof framing. Expert craftsmen from New York cut and installed each of the more than 10,000 tin-dipped, stainless-steel shingles for the roof. Lead workers came from Toronto, Canada, to install lead flashing around the chimneys and over basement windows. Craftsmen on staff used an adze to make oak lintels for the door and window openings.

Restorers used salvaged antique heart pine for the terras roof, ordered reproduction crown glass for the windows from Germany, and hemp window sash cord from Holland.

In searching for the best materials and craftspeople, modern restorers have shown great patience and perseverance, much like Jefferson himself.

Computer Mapping and Lab Analysis

Many archaeological discoveries take place in the laboratory, where artifacts are cleaned, identified, catalogued, and analyzed. Lab research can reveal how artifacts were made and used, where they came from, and even how much they might have cost.

Analysis can also be used to create computer maps that show the variations in artifact types and frequencies across a site, revealing new information. At a slave quarter site excavated at Poplar Forest, for example, artifact maps showed where people spent the most time working, where they deposited their trash, and where they may have hung laundry to dry. All of these clues help us to understand how people used space in the past, and challenge us to explain why they did what they did. In this case, evidence suggests that people chose to spend time working and socializing on the side of their cabin that faced away from the overseer's house. Thus, artifact analysis has helped us to understand issues of privacy.

Poplar Forest Today

As Poplar Forest is reshaped before our eyes back to the way Jefferson wanted it to be, it calls up his great ghost in ever more palpable form . . . making the restoration the most moving event, for me, in recent architectural history.

—VINCENT J. SCULLY, JR.,
ARCHITECTURAL HISTORIAN

Jefferson once suggested to a friend, "You must come with your ears stuffed

The remnant found in the sand bed of the central fireplace.

Two exciting discoveries of artifacts from unusual sources were found in the house during investigation. One cache represented artifacts spanning 1809–1845. Workers rebuilding the house in 1846 needed a sand bed in which to place the new hearthstones of the central room fireplace. For expediency, they simply took a pile of plaster from house fire debris and crushed it up for its sand content. They never bothered to remove the other parts, which contained a treasure trove of wood, glass, metal, and other materials, providing clues to the house's construction. Included in this material were two pieces of the Doric and Ionic entablature friezes, confirming the design and that they were made of baked clay, painted white, and installed in parts with screws. An additional bonus came from uncrushed plaster pieces. Paint analysis determined seven different wall colors from the house, all but one composed of pigmented lime washes.

The second discovery contained artifacts from 1847 into the 1960s. Found in the hollow spaces of post-Jefferson walls and floors were numerous rat nests. These helpful collectors had sampled everyday life in and around the house for more than one hundred years. Examples of cloth, wood, food, games, letters, newspapers, and many other items inform us what the inhabitants were eating, wearing, reading, growing on the farm, playing, making, and purchasing.

full of cotton to fortify them against the noise of hammers, saws, planes, etc. which assail us in every direction." The same advice could sometimes apply today as Poplar Forest buzzes with the activity of craftspeople restoring the house.

But Poplar Forest today is also tranquil, a place to discover Jefferson on a personal scale—his ideals for his private life, the challenges he faced, and how he renewed his creativity.

The Visitor Experience

Poplar Forest is a rarity: visitors have an unhurried opportunity to get to know the private side of Thomas Jefferson within the fabric of his time. They get to know his family and learn about his plantation. Poplar Forest also offers the visitor a deep understanding of how Jefferson shaped his personal environment and expressed his ideals in his architecture and landscape.

Work areas are also open to the public, so they might see a mason laying brick or a carpenter installing trim just as Jefferson's own craftsmen did. Visitors might witness archaeologists at work as well, discovering how they learn about the past, not just what they learn. Visitors can sit in reproductions of Jefferson's Windsor chairs, try to write with a reproduction of his polygraph, and even experience the same quiet that Jefferson himself would have.

Involvement

Work on Poplar Forest's revival also continues outside of Virginia through friends organizations in many cities. These friends work to spread the word

Visitors to Poplar Forest today can participate in hands-on activities.

Guided tours are offered daily during the visitation season.

about Poplar Forest and the need for funds to support ongoing work to preserve this national landmark. The funds raised go to restore and maintain the buildings and grounds, buy back property containing important archaeological sites, keep Poplar Forest open to the public, and build an endowment to ensure its preservation for future generations. Support from many people has brought Poplar Forest this far. Involvement is the key to continuing the archaeological and architectural discoveries at Poplar Forest and to fully achieving the rescue of Jefferson's retreat.

■ In Poplar Forest's hands-on history area, children make bricks as they were made in Jefferson's time.

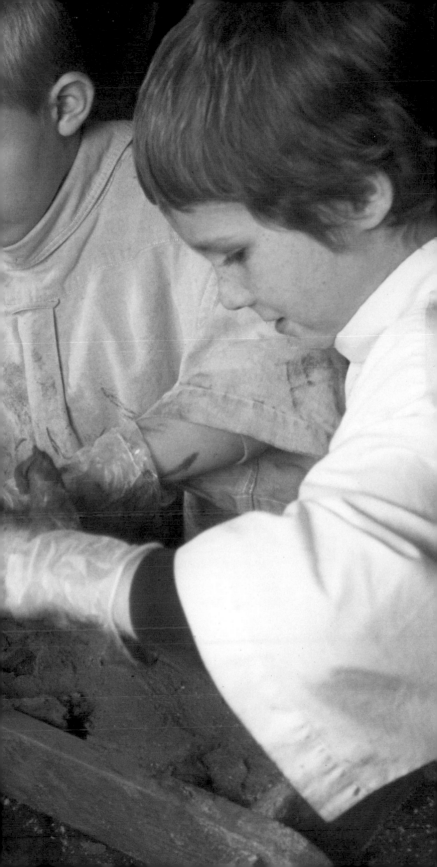

Books about Thomas Jefferson

William Howard Adams, *The Eye of Thomas Jefferson*, 1981

Noble E. Cunningham, Jr., *In Pursuit of Reason: The Life of Thomas Jefferson*, 1987

Joseph J. Ellis, *American Sphinx: The Character of Thomas Jefferson*, 1996

Dumas Malone, *Thomas Jefferson: A Brief Biography*, 1993

Dumas Malone, *Jefferson and His Time* (6 vols.), *1948-1981*

Jack McLaughlin, *Jefferson and Monticello: The Biography of a Builder*, 1988

Susan Stein, *The Worlds of Thomas Jefferson at Monticello*, 1993

Jefferson's Writings

Edwin Morris Betts, ed., *Thomas Jefferson's Farm Book*, 1953, rpt. 1976

Edwin Morris Betts, ed., *Thomas Jefferson's Garden Book*, 1944, rpt. 1985

Julian P. Boyd and others, eds., *The Papers of Thomas Jefferson*, (29 vols., currently through February 1797), 1950–present

William Peden, ed., *Notes on the State of Virginia*, 1954, rpt. 1982

Merrill D. Peterson, ed., *Thomas Jefferson: Writings*, 1984

Books about Slavery

Lawrence B. Goodheart and others, eds., *Slavery in American Society*, 3rd ed., 1993

Peter Kolchin, *American Slavery 1619-1877*, 1994

Lucia C. Stanton, *Slavery at Monticello*, 1996

Lucia C. Stanton, *Free Some Day: The African American Families of Monticello*, 2000

Selected Articles about Poplar Forest

C. Allan Brown, "Poplar Forest, The Mathematics of an Ideal Villa," *Journal of Garden History* (1990)

S. Allen Chambers, Jr., "Poplar Forest, Jefferson's Hermitage," *Antiques* (July 1993)

Jane Brown Gillette, "Mr. Jefferson's Retreat," *Historic Preservation* (July/August, 1992)

Travis McDonald, "Poplar Forest, A Masterpiece Rediscovered," *Virginia Cavalcade* (Winter, 1993)

Travis McDonald, "Privacy Restored: Thomas Jefferson's Poplar Forest," *Virginia Cavalcade* (Winter, 2002)

Travis McDonald, "Constructing Optimism: Thomas Jefferson's Poplar Forest," *People, Power, Places,* 2000

Books about Poplar Forest

S. Allen Chambers, Jr., *Poplar Forest and Thomas Jefferson*, 1993

Barbara J. Heath, *Hidden Lives: The Archaeology of Slave Life at Thomas Jefferson's Poplar Forest*, 1999

Books for Children and Youth

David A. Adler, *A Picture Book of Thomas Jefferson*, 1990

Marvin Barrett, *Meet Thomas Jefferson*, 1989

Natalie S. Bober, *Thomas Jefferson, Man on a Mountain*, 1988

Roger Bruns, *Thomas Jefferson*, World Leaders Past and Present Series, 1986

Sheryl Kingery Mays, *Explore Poplar Forest: Thomas Jefferson's Retreat*, 2000

Acknowledgments

On behalf of the Board of Directors, I would like to thank all who contributed to ensure the quality and accuracy of this journey through Poplar Forest.

This book was truly a team effort. First, acknowledgment must go to S. Allen Chambers, whose book *Poplar Forest and Thomas Jefferson* laid the foundation for this work. In addition, the research by Dr. Barbara Heath, Poplar Forest's Director of Archaeology and Landscapes, and Travis McDonald, Director of Architectural Restoration, and their staffs have dramatically increased our knowledge of Poplar Forest. This book was conceived and shepherded through every phase of its development by a dedicated committee of Poplar Forest staff

The Corporation for Jefferson's Poplar Forest wishes to thank the following institutions and individuals for granting permission to use illustrations and photos in this publication: Lynn A. Beebe – 131; Barbara J. Heath – 51, 53 (inset) 57-58, 100; Mrs. Edwin C. Hutter – 110; Diane Johnson – inside front cover illustration; Doug Koontz – 133-134; Travis McDonald – 7; 13; 23-24; 32; 34; 36; 39; 41; 42; 46; 61-62; 69; 115; 121; 123; 124; 125; 129-130; Gail McIntosh – inside back cover illustration; John I Mesick – 33; Edmund Potter – 103-104; Les Schofer – cover (front), 2, 3-4, 10, 35, 47-48, 63-64, 79-80, 89-90, 99, 102, 105, 106, 107, 113-114; Karin Sherbin – 132; Jackson Smith – cover (front), cover (back), 7, 13, 15, 25-26, 27, 31, 33, 40, 49-50, 51, 57 (inset), 60, 65-66, 67, 73, 78, 87-88, 111-112, 126, 135-136; By Permission of Ellen Eddy Thorndike and Elizabeth Eddy Cornwall – 82; Robert Zeigler – 27; American Philosophical Society – 70; Colonial Williamsburg Foundation – 60 (inset); Library of Congress – 11, 12, 22, 85-86, 98; Florida State Photo Archives, Tallahassee, Florida –117 (inset); Courtesy of the Fogg Art Museum, Harvard University Art Museums, Gift of Mrs. T. Jefferson Newbold and family, in memory of Thomas Jefferson Newbold, Class of 1910, Photo courtesy of Rick Stafford, Copyright President and Fellows of Harvard College – back cover portrait; The Corporation for Jefferson's Poplar Forest – 54, 56, 67, 71, 77, 91, 101, 115; 117; 119 (inset), 127, 128;

Robert, Hubert (1733-1808), *La Maison Carree à Nimes,* oil on canvas, 243 x 244 cm, Copyright Erich Lessing / Art Resource, NY, Louvre, Paris, Photo Courtesy of Erich Lessing / Art Resource, NY – 19; Courtesy of the Massachusetts Historical Society – 30 (inset), 76, 94; Mesick Cohen Wilson Baker Architects – 30, 31, 37-38, 43-44, 45; Monticello/Thomas Jefferson Foundation, Inc. – 11, 16, 17, 18, 21, 55, 61, 70, 72, 74, 83, 84, 86, 97; Print Collection, Miriam and Ira D. Wallach Division of Art, Prints and Photographs, The New York Public Library, Astor, Lenox and Tilden Foundations – 59; Rare Books Division, The New York Public Library, Astor, Lenox and Tilden Foundations - 6; Stuart Collection, Rare Books Division, The New York Public Library, Astor, Lenox and Tilden Foundations – 91; Virginia Historical Society, Richmond, Virginia – 28; Courtesy of University of Virginia Art Museum, Gift of Thomas Fortune Ryan, 1912.1 Collection, Frederic Edwin Church, *The Natural Bridge, Virginia*, 1852 – 74; Thomas Jefferson Papers, University of Virginia Library – 13, 53; O'Neil, William Bainter. *Jefferson's Fine Arts Library.* Charlottesville, University of Virginia Press, 1976, The Albert and Shirley Small Special Collections Library, University of Virginia Library – 29; The Library of Virginia – 12, 119-120; Fréat de Chambray. *Parallel de l'architecture antique avec la moderne,* 1766. Rare Books Division, Special Collections, University of Virginia Library – 33.

chaired by Octavia Starbuck, Director of Interpretation and Education. The team included Suzan Bryan, Dianne Kinney, Gail Pond, and Karin Sherbin, in addition to Dr. Heath and Mr. McDonald.

I would like to extend sincere thanks also to the following individuals whose skills contributed so much to this book: writer Joan L. Horn; Lisa Ross and Tom van der Voort of Payne Ross Associates who helped plan and produce the book; designer Jeremy Crenshaw of Payne Ross; and copyeditor Gail Wiley.

Special thanks are extended to English Construction, Wolf Branch Farm, and Woodburne Farm.

Lynn A. Beebe
Executive Director

Main Level

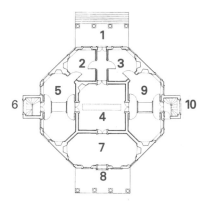

1. North Portico
2. Northwest Room
   Storage/Spare Bedroom
3. Northeast Room
   Storage/Spare Bedroom
4. Dining Room
5. West Bedroom
   Jefferson's Bedroom
6. West Stair Pavilion
7. Parlor (South Room)
8. South Portico
9. East Bedroom
   Grandchildren's Bedroom
10. East Stair Pavilion

Lower Level

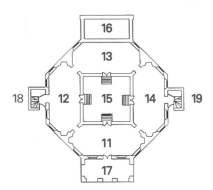

11. Unfinished Room
12. Unfinished Room
13. Unfinished Room
14. Unfinished Room
15. Cellar–Wine, Cider,
    Brandy & Beer Storage
16. Non-Historic Area
    Mechanical Room
17. Arcade
18. West Stair Pavilion
19. East Stair Pavilion

Wing of Offices

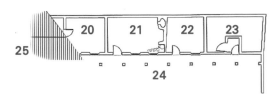

20. Cold Storage
21. Kitchen
22. Cook's Room / Laundry

23. Smokehouse
24. Covered Walkway
25. Terras Roof